TEACHINGS OF SILVER BIRCH

Edited by
A. W. AUSTEN

Foreword by
HANNEN SWAFFER

"This book goes out into the world of matter with the blessing of the world of spirit. I pray that each whom it reaches may have his eyes opened and his soul touched, for until the soul is quickened and is aware of the higher, deeper, nobler and greater things of life, the individual is living in a mist."

– SILVER BIRCH

The Spiritual Truth Press

First published in 1938
Eleventh impression 2006

Spiritual Truth Press
15 Broom Hall, Oxshott
Surrey KT22 0JZ

ISBN 0 85384 102 0

Printed in Great Britain by Booksprint

INTRODUCTION

There are a number of possible reasons why you are reading this book. The first and most likely is that you are already a "follower" of Silver Birch and have found his great wisdom and spiritual insights of benefit in your life. In this case you will welcome this reprint of one of the classic books of his teachings. Maybe you have been given this book by a friend who believes its message of love, in this world and in the next, will inspire or comfort you. If so, you will not be disappointed.

Perhaps you chanced upon it on a bookshelf or saw it advertised, then curiosity got the better of you. Well, after reading its pages you may also decide that "chance" played no part in the decision and that some form of spiritual guidance has brought you and this book together.

Whatever the reason, the chances are that Silver Birch's wisdom will remain with you forever. Long after you have forgotten his precise words, his guidance will still be a very real influence whenever you need it. And if you need to jog your memory – just reach for this book and read it again. Silver Birch's words are so accessible and meaningful that you will never tire of reading them. But who is Silver Birch, the spirit guide whose words are faithfully recorded here? And who was Maurice Barbanell, the London medium who channelled that wisdom? Without an answer to these questions, many new readers – however impressed with these teachings – will be puzzled about their source.

Barbanell was the founder and editor of a weekly Spiritualist newspaper, *Psychic News*, and for half a century devoted his life to spreading spiritual knowledge through its columns and those of other publications with which he was associated. In his own obituary, which he wrote before his passsing at the age of 79 on July 17th 1981, he revealed that he was told by Estelle Roberts' Red Cloud – a spirit guide for whom he had the greatest admiration – that in a previous incarnation he had made a promise to reincarnate and devote his life to spreading Spiritualism. Though he had no knowlege of that life or promise, events certainly conspired to make it possible.

He was born to Jewish parents in a poor area of London's East End. His mother was devoutly religious but his father, a barber, was an atheist so Barbanell heard many arguments about religion during his early years. His father always won, and his son adopted the same outlook but later changed to agnosticism. Yet after hearing about Spiritualism from a speaker at a social and literary club of which he was secretary, Barbanell refused to start the debate by putting an opposing view – one of his duties – because, he explained, he had made no personal investigation and therefore his opinions were valueless. This impressed the speaker who invited Barbanell to attend a séance in which a medium, Mrs Blaustein, was entranced by various spirits of different nationalities. He was not impressed, and on a second visit fell asleep. Barbanell apologised, believing that either boredom or tiredness had been responsible, but the other circle members informed him that he had not been asleep but had been in trance and a Red Indian had spoken through him.

With the encouragement of famous Fleet Street journalist Hannen Swaffer, Barbanell founded *Psychic News* partly as a vehicle for the guide's teachings. But, because he knew he would be criticised for publishing his own mediumship in his own newspaper, Barbanell did not reveal to his readers for many years who was channelling the wisdom, by which time the guide had a huge following on his own merits.

Silver Birch spoke regularly at Barbanell's home circle and the proceedings were always recorded in shorthand. There were a number of differences in style and procedure between Barbabell's own journalistic efforts and the way in which Silver Birch communicated, as Barbanell himself observed.

"In my working life I use words every day. I have never yet written or dictated an article with which I was satisfied when I read it. Inevitably I find, when looking at the typed material, that I can improve it by altering words, phrases and sentences. No such problem arises with the guide's teachings. These flow pefectly, requiring usually only punctuation. Another interesting aspect is the occasional use of words that I regard as arhaic and do not form part of my normal vocabulary."

But who was Silver Birch? A psychic artist depicts him as a serious-looking native American Indian with a single feather and compassionate eyes. There is evidence to suggest that this was simply a convenient persona behind which a far more spiritually evolved soul hid in order that those who read his words would judge them not by the name attached to them but by the wisdom that pervades every sentence.

Those of us who knew them both were well aware of the differences in the way they spoke and the words they used. They both had spiritual missions and they fulfilled them admirably, particularly when working together in their two-world partnership. This, as you are about to discover, has provided us with simple, uplifting, comforting and inspirational answers to the questions we all ask from time to time, about life and its purpose. They are needed now more than ever before as we prepare for the challenges which will confront us in the 21st century.

Roy Stemman
Chairman
Spiritual Truth Foundation

CONTENTS

FOREWORD

By HANNEN SWAFFER

SILVER BIRCH, as we call him, is not a Red Indian. Who he is, we do not know. We assume that he uses the name of the spirit through whose astral body he expresses himself, it being impossible for the high vibration of the spiritual realm to which he belongs to manifest except through some other instrument.

He is the spirit guide of what is known as "HANNEN SWAFFER'S HOME CIRCLE."

"One day I will tell you who I am," he told us recently. "I had to come in the form of a humble Indian to win your love and devotion, not by the use of any high-sounding name, and to prove myself by the truth of what I taught. That is the Law."

Once, he nearly gave himself away, for, in describing his mission, in the words used in his own story, printed on Page 17, he began: "They said to me. . . . I nearly used my real name then."

Now Silver Birch came into my life soon after I became a Spiritualist in 1924. Ever since then, I have listened, for an hour and more at a time, to his teaching, his guidance and his counsel, and learned to love and respect him more than I love and respect any earthly being.

He first functioned in an extraordinary way. A young man of eighteen, an Atheist who was making a study of Spiritualism, went mockingly to a circle in one of the poorest of

London's suburbs. He laughed outright when, to use his own words, "old women became Chinamen and all sorts of things," only to be reproved by a medium who, in trance, said: "*You will be doing this before long.*"

Although he went away incredulous and sceptical, he returned the next week to the circle and then, half-way through, apologized for having fallen asleep.

"You have been in trance," said someone sitting next to him. "Your guide gave his name and said that he has been training you for this for years and that, before long, you will be speaking on Spiritualist platforms."

Again, the young man laughed. . . .

In those days, Silver Birch spoke very few words of English, and those with a very crude accent. As the years passed, for he began to control his new-found medium often, his knowledge of our language so improved that his simple eloquence now often transcends that of any speaker to whom I have ever listened.

'How do you know that the medium was in trance?" I have been asked.

On more than one occasion Silver Birch, speaking through his medium, has told us to stick a pin in the medium's hand, and then to stick it in deeper. When coming out of trance, the medium has not remembered feeling anything. Nor has any mark been visible.

"How do you know it does not come from the medium's subconscious mind?" is another question. Well, in some ways, the two contradict each other. Silver Birch teaches Reincarnation. The medium himself turns down this theory and yet, in trance, confounds himself.

Then another curious little thing is the fact that until, so that the guide's words could be printed in *Psychic News*, a reporter started to take them down, the medium always remembered, just as he was going to sleep that night, what had been said while he was in trance. This was because, when consenting to be a medium, he had extracted from Silver Birch a promise that he would know what had been said. Directly we started to record it, all this stopped.

Now, the medium reads, next morning, the report of the sitting and is amazed at the beauty of the language that is uttered through his lips.

Silver Birch is a teacher. He does not heal. He seldom gives evidential messages. Now and then, he apologizes for that, saying that he often regrets that he confined his mastery of the medium to teaching. Although he regards this teaching as all-important, he recognizes that the world needs evidence of Survival.

During recent years, I have taken all sorts of people to hear Silver Birch talk—ministers of religion, journalists, people from all parts of the world. I have never heard from any one of them a word of criticism of anything he said.

One parson who took to him his theological difficulties found himself reduced to silence when, in simple words, Silver Birch explained what he calls "the Law".

"Write down the most difficult questions you can think of," I had said to the minister, beforehand. He went along, eager to challenge one of those spirit guides he had heard so often condemned by men of his cloth. He came away confounded. Silver Birch had made difficult theology too simple for a theologian.

Now my home circle, of whom Silver Birch is the guide, sits every Friday night. Regularly every week, *Psychic News* prints a verbatim record of what he says. It is given to our home circle not for our private use, but so that it can be broadcast right across the world.

As a consequence, Silver Birch has more followers than any earthly preacher. They belong to every clime and to almost every race, and are people of all shades of colour.

Yet, put down in cold print, Silver Birch's words cannot do more than convey a little of the nobility of his character, the warmth of his friendship and the natural dignity of his utterance. Sometimes, they compel tears. We know that we are in the presence, however humbly he may speak, of a high, exalted spirit. He never reproves. He never finds fault.

The Churches talk of Jesus of Nazareth, of whom they know little, and of whose existence they have no proof. Silver Birch talks of "The Nazarene", as he calls him, as the highest of all the spiritual beings with whom he has contact, and, as Silver Birch has proved to us, after years of close association, that he could not lie, we know, if only because he says so, that the Jesus of the New Testament is still functioning, still engaged on that divine mission which once brought him to this earth. So, to us, the words, "Lo, I am with you alway, even unto the end of the world," have a meaning which the Churches cannot explain.

When, in the pages which follow, you read Silver Birch's teaching, you must understand that it is all written down in the dark by a reporter who uses Braille notepaper, and who, expert stenographer though he is, is often tested severely to keep pace with the rapidity of Silver Birch's speech. On no occasion has a single word to be altered. Silver Birch's words flow in perfect English. Only the punctuation marks have to be put in, and even for these there is always a natural place which could not be mistaken.

Silver Birch's philosophy, as you will easily understand, is that of a Pantheist, a man who realizes that God is found in Nature itself, that there is an unalterable Law which governs everything, and that God is the Law.

"You are within the Great Spirit," says Silver Birch, "and the Great Spirit is within you." So we learn we are all potential gods, part of the great creative principle which is Everything.

Yet Silver Birch does not stop at unapplied philosophy. He forces home, always, the lesson that we are here to do a job. He sums up religion in the one word "Service," and strives to teach us, clumsy instruments though we may be, that we are in this world so that we may make an end of war, abolish poverty and hasten the time when God's bounty will be spread in all its lavishness among all the peoples of the world.

"Our allegiance," says Silver Birch, "is not to a Creed, not to a Book, not to a Church, but to the Great Spirit of Life and to His eternal natural laws."

So it is that the members of his circle, six in number, include three Jews and three Gentiles, who find in Spiritualism no racial or creedal difference. Three were Agnostics and a fourth was a Wesleyan minister who, just before he joined our circle, had left Methodism because no longer could he accept its teachings.

Sometimes, to vary the sittings, Silver Birch allows some other spirit to control his medium. So we have been visited by Northcliffe, Galsworthy, Hall Caine, Gilbert Parker, Horace Greeley, Dick Sheppard, Abraham Lincoln and personal friends of the sitters. Still, all that is for another book. . . .

During my years of sitting with Silver Birch, I have never known him to forget anything, although we may do so.

And never, by any syllable, does he depart from his self-chosen mission to instruct the children of men in a simpler and more beneficent way of life.

EDITOR'S NOTE

THESE teachings from Silver Birch—he insists that he is not the author, but the messenger through whom they are relayed from higher sources—are not put forward as the infallible utterances of a being possessed of all wisdom. It is not the object of spirit intercourse that we should denude ourselves of the critical faculty and accept blindly the words of another, whether in this world or the next. Nor is it the desire to create a new Orthodoxy, for revelation is progressive and is dependent on our capacity to receive it.

The appeal of Silver Birch is to Reason, and if anything he says is not acceptable to the reader's reason then it should be rejected or at least left as an open question pending further evidence.

To make the book more useful for reference, I have selected from the reports of hundreds of sittings the teachings of the guide on each specific subject. It should not be assumed that each chapter is a report of one long, connected speech. It may be composed of extracts from Silver Birch's remarks spread over thirty or forty séances.

It has been my task to group these extracts in such a way as to preserve continuity of thought throughout the treatment of each subject. For the further convenience of the reader, except in the last two chapters, I have used **black** type for all editorial references and *italic* type for all questions submitted to the guide. The remarks of Silver Birch, and his replies to questions, are printed throughout in the more common type known as Roman.

March, 1938. A. W. AUSTEN.

SILVER BIRCH'S OWN STORY

Here, Silver Birch tells in his own words of the long struggle he had before he was able to transmit his message:

WHEN I was asked, many long years ago, whether I would return to the world of matter and find on earth a band who would work with me to deliver the message of the spirit, I said I would, as did many others, and my task was given me.

I was told that I would have to search and find an instrument and so attach myself to this instrument that I would be able to express through him the message that I was charged to deliver. So I searched our records and found my medium.

I watched from the time that he was conceived, and from the moment that the spirit began to express itself—albeit as a little flicker—I brought my influence to bear and started there and then this association which has lasted all these years.

I helped to mould the spirit and the tiny little mind and throughout every phase of that life I watched his every experience, learned how to get a close association and I accustomed myself throughout the days of boyhood to all the mental processes, to all the physical habits. I studied my instrument from every aspect—mind, spirit and physical body.

And then I had to guide his footsteps towards an understanding of these spirit truths. First, I guided him to make a study of the many religions in your world of matter, until his mind revolted and he began to be what your world calls an

Atheist. And when that had played its part in the mental unfoldment, he was ready for me to begin my task of speaking through his lips.

I guided him to his first meeting. I helped to bring him to his first circle. And there, in the power provided, I made my first contact—so crude, so trivial, but from my point of view so important—and I uttered my first expression in the world of matter through another's organism.

From that day I learned how to obtain better and better control, until now you see the result. We have achieved so much that I can register the totality of my ideas and eliminate for all purposes what is in the medium's own personality.

Now I would like to tell you something about my mission. They said to me: "You will have to go into the world of matter and, when you have found your instrument, you will have to bring to him sympathetic souls who will aid you to deliver your message." I searched and found you all and brought you together.

But the greatest difficulty I had to face was that I had to make the choice whether I would return to provide those proofs that your world must have to satisfy itself—material proofs, I mean, not spiritual ones, for your world does not understand those—or whether I would return as a teacher and teach truth. I chose the harder.

I said that, after all those long years, with all the manifold experiences I had had in the realms of spirit, I would return and try to appeal with love to those whom I would strive to teach. I would appeal to reason. I would appeal to the judgment of mature, evolved and what you call educated minds. I would reveal the message of the spirit in all its simplicity.

I would say nothing that offended reason. I would strive to manifest love, never to reproach with anger, but to appeal always with love, and prove by precept and example and by all I did that I was what I claimed to be—a messenger of the Great Spirit.

And I imposed upon myself the burden of anonymity, so that I would make no appeal of illustrious personage, title, rank, or fame, but would be judged on what I said and what I did. When I was in the spheres at the last festival they praised me and said I had accomplished much of my mission. And tears of joy fell down my face. But my mission is not yet over. There is still more to be done.

Because of the work that others have done—the same work that we do—there is more light in your world of matter, there is more happiness, there is less sorrow, less tears. We have won a partial victory over the grave.

We have inspired many to let their higher selves rise in their lives. We have driven out many of the falsehoods of the past that have blinded men's eyes to justice and truth. We have helped to free many from the prison-house of creed and dogma which has afflicted your world for so many years, shaming reason with its foolish stupidities.

We have sought—and succeeded in some measure—to teach of a Great Spirit of love and wisdom, not of partiality, not or wrath, not vindictive and angry, not a dealer of pestilence and disease. We have sought to reveal the Nazarene as a great exemplar. And many have seen the reason that lies in our teaching.

Great work has been done, but a greater work still has to be done. There is war in your world of matter, war that need not be, for if your world knew these truths and lived them, men would not kill. There is starvation, when there is plenty of the Great Spirit's bounty. There are mean hovels where the children of the Great Spirit are compelled to live, deprived of fresh air, unable to catch the health-giving rays of the sun, forced to live below the line of sustenance. There is want and distress and misery.

There are still superstitions to be killed. There are still aching hearts. There are still diseases to be vanquished. Our task is not yet complete. We rejoice at the work that has been done and pray that strength shall be given to us so that, with your co-operation, we may be enabled to render greater service still.

* * * * *

I am only the mouthpiece of those who sent me, and I seek no glory for myself and no reward. I have no desire to aggrandize myself or my personality. I rejoice to be a vehicle for expressing these truths, lost for many centuries and now restored to the world of matter, stamped with the seal of divine truth.

My part is that of the messenger who speaks the message and I have striven to be faithful and to convey that which was given to me according to the instrument that I have and the power which I have earned. I only want to be of service and, if the few teachings I express help one soul to find peace in a stormy life, to find the shelter of truth after having experienced the storms of doubt, if within the sanctuary of these simple spiritual truths one can find happiness and be inspired to serve, then perhaps we have accomplished something of the Father's work.

WHY SPIRIT GUIDES RETURN

Why should those in the spirit world trouble to come back to enlighten us on earth? It is because they know that the world needs their message more than it needs anything else. Here, Silver Birch explains why he has returned to teach us:

LIKE many others, I was asked whether I would go back into the belt of matter to try to save those in your world who were trying to destroy themselves and the world in which they lived. We have tried to work amongst you, and we still try to work amongst you, seeking by your own standards to prove that those who leave your world still live in the fuller realms of the Great Spirit, so that you shall understand that you are part of the Great Spirit even as they are.

Although we strive in these things, there are many who seem to think it is more important to worry about the toys than the message. What does it matter whether the message comes from one whom the world calls white, or black, or yellow, or red? What does it matter if the laws of the Great Spirit are given you by one who has had much education or not, so long as it is the Law, so long as it is the truth?

Many years ago, you were taught that "A little child shall lead them." Until you learn to put away the foolish wisdom of the wise, and get back to the simplicity of the child, you will not advance much either in your world or in mine. Your world makes a difference between those whose skins have been coloured by the sun of the Great Spirit. They look at their skins and forget that their spirits are all one.

Why do you think you have wars? Why do you think you have misery? Why do you think you have great sorrow in your world? Because those who are blinded by matter and can only see through its limitations do not see that behind the things of matter there is a unifying spirit of the Great Spirit. Because they seek to make differences, they have chaos, they have disaster, they have bankruptcy.

I have told you before, it is we whom you call the "savage" Indians that have been brought back, as part of the Law of the Great Spirit, to try to teach you the laws that your civilization has forgotten. You have sought to build your lives on the systems of your own material world. You have sought to become educated and cultured and have tried to build up a civilization away from the laws of the Great Spirit.

Because of that, your world has fallen. It is in ruins, just as much in ruins as is the civilization of the olden days. Because we love you, because that love which comes from the Great Spirit flows through all of us, we come back to you to try to help you to pick up the pieces and build them on the structure of eternal things, the laws of the Great Spirit.

Because when we lived on earth we had coloured skins, you say to us: "No, we refuse to have the world put right because your skin is coloured. We would rather have disaster, unless we can be helped by people whose skins are white."

But, all the same, I want you to know that you help us. There is much in the things that you have discovered in your own civilization that helps us. It is a perfect law in its operation. We seek to teach you what we have learned in the realms of spirit, and we seek to imbibe whatever knowledge you can give us. It is through that law of co-operation that the new heaven will come into your world.

One day in your world all the colours will merge, for all the colours have their part to play. All peoples will merge, because each has something to give to the world. You can see the time coming, if you look with the eyes of the spirit, when all will live together in harmony, giving all peoples the advantage of their own race, their own culture and their own learning.

We are all servants of the Great Spirit—you and I and those who work with us—seeking to do His will. We are misunderstood; often our friends are our greatest enemies. But we do our work and, because we do that which is right in the sight of the Great Spirit, we call to our aid all those forces which belong to the spirit, which are stronger than your world of matter. And gradually good triumphs over evil, justice triumphs over injustice, and right triumphs over wrong. Sometimes the forces of your world push us back for a while, but not for ever.

We must succeed, for we seek to save mankind from himself, to point to him those higher and better ways which will enable him to live his life in service, so that he may receive the richness of soul, spirit and mind, the peace and the happiness which do not belong to the world of matter but to the higher and greater things of the spirit.

It is a great task on which we are all engaged. It is a sacred tie that binds us all together and makes us one in spirit, one in purpose, one in desire. Let us resolve that together we will renew our opposition to all that which stands in the way of Truth's advance, so that our combined efforts bring the power of the Great Spirit nearer to His children.

If the few words I say are of service to you, then they should enable each one of you to go out into the world and serve the children of matter as I try to serve you. It is your responsibility to pass on the knowledge you have. I know that to be the Law.

I only seek to interpret into your language the laws of the Great Spirit. Those who read my words will not always agree with my interpretations, but I am in a different world from them. I am sometimes limited by your language and by my instrument. If we fail to agree, then it is either because the souls in your world are not yet evolved to an understanding of greater truths, or because I cannot express all that is within my soul, which is greater than your earthly language allows me to interpret.

But I am always ready to serve and to teach the Law, for it is only through an understanding of the laws of the Great Spirit that the people of the world of matter can live as the Great Spirit intended they should live. It is better to see than to be blind, it is better to hear than to be deaf, it is better to be awake than to be asleep. Let them open their souls to the Great Spirit. Let them strive to attune themselves to the laws of the Great Spirit, so that they are at one with Him and He is at one with them.

Then their hearts and souls will be at peace, they will be in harmony with the great rhythm of the universe, and discord will disappear from their lives. They will begin to live as they have never lived before.

All knowledge matters. It is not wise to say you will only receive this amount of knowledge and will go no further.

I strive to transmit all I know so that you may drink in as much as I have to give you. I do this not because I am greater than you, not because I am proud of what I possess, but because only by giving can I serve.

All knowledge has its place. Do not strive to stop at any rung in the ladder of progress. It is only by imbibing, by striving to get the complete picture, that life will be understood by you.

That refers not only to life in its material aspects, but life in its spiritual aspects, too, for whilst your world of matter needs guidance in the things of matter it is also necessary for the knowledge of the spirit to be given at the same time. Our message always is that you are living now in the world of spirit, that the world of matter is but one reflection of an eternal life.

If only those who know would be faithful to the knowledge, how much more could we accomplish? If only those who have listened to the voice of the spirit and those who have witnessed the operation of spiritual laws in the phenomena that links together the two worlds of life would forget Self and rise to the highest heights that they could scale, we could achieve a great deal.

Knowledge and service are greater than individuals. What we have achieved is but little compared with what can be achieved. No limits can be set to the Great Infinite Spirit, to the wisdom, to the inspiration, to the truth that can be showered upon your world. There are no restrictions to the mighty power of spirit waiting to fill your world, when your instruments can provide the right channels for us to use.

THE DIVINE PLAN

Silver Birch here explains something of the plan that is behind spirit communication:

OUR work is to give that which has a purpose, a significance, so that, while it demonstrates the existence of Law, it also enables comfort to be given and knowledge to be spread. Our work is not only to reveal the existence of laws beyond the physical, but to reveal truths of the spirit.

We have a gigantic system of misrepresentation to oppose. We have to undo the work of centuries. We have to destroy the superstructure of falsity that has been built upon the foundations of creeds.

We are striving always to teach the children of matter how to be free and how to bask in the sunlight of spiritual truth, how to cast off the serfdom of creedal slavery. That is not an easy task, for once the trappings of religion have mastered you, it takes a long time for spiritual truth to penetrate that thick wall of superstition.

We strive always to reveal the religious significance of spiritual truth, for, when your world understands its spiritual import, there will be a revolution mightier than all the revolutions of war and blood.

It will be a revolution of the soul and, all over the world, people will claim what is their due—the right to enjoy to the full the liberties of the spirit. Away will go every restriction which has put fetters on them.

Our allegiance is not to a Creed, not to a Book, not to a

Church, but to the Great Spirit of life and to His eternal natural laws.

A great power of the spirit will descend into your world of matter. In all its countries a mighty force of the spirit will be felt, for there is a great work to be done to counteract the selfishness and the ignorance of your world. In time it will conquer, but, in the process, there will be much travail.

Plenty of workers have come to take their stand at your side.

There are those who are known to you, those who are bound to you with ties of blood and others who are attracted to serve you out of the love that they bear for you. When you think of those whose names you know, try to realize the countless host of the unknown, who serve without any desire to be known or recognized but who give their power to be used.

The world will not be converted in a blinding flash like Saul on the road to Damascus. Gradually, the light of spiritual truths will break through, as more people become aware of the great knowledge and more instruments are available for the power of the Great White Spirit to use.

You must remember that the things of the spirit require careful nurture and progress. Sudden conversions would not be enduring, and our work is intended to be permanent.

Each soul that becomes an instrument for the Great Spirit, each soul that moves out of darkness into the light, out of ignorance into knowledge, out of superstition into truth, is helping to advance the world, for each one of these is a nail that is driven into the coffin of the world's materialism.

What you must all learn is that there are two forms of development. You can unfold that which is of the soul and you can unfold that which is of the spirit. One is the development of only the psychic faculty, and the other is soul-growth.

Where you get the development of the psychic without the spiritual, there you have a low plane of vibration. When you get a combination of both, then you have not only a great medium, but a great man or woman.

What a glorious message we have for your world of matter—a message that makes men free and teaches them to rejoice in their divine heritage; a message that teaches them to throw off all shackles and bonds: a message that teaches them to rejoice in the fulness of spiritual knowledge; a message that shows them how to live not only on the planes of matter, but on the planes of spirit; a message that brings them beauty, love and wisdom, understanding, truth and happiness; a message that speaks of service, service, service.

And yet we are denied by those who do not understand the revelation of the Great Spirit and who deny the spirit, as the power of the spirit has been denied throughout all times.

The work that we do becomes more and more necessary. Your world is full of bloodshed, tears of misery and bitterness. In its blindness, your world will not live according to the laws of the Great Spirit. It has chosen the path that leads to darkness and to despair.

We offer the knowledge that leads to hope, to light, to peace and to harmony. Your world may despise us, in its ignorance. It may reject the message that we bring. It may deny the power that accompanies us. But our great truth must prevail, for it is of the Great Spirit.

Those who strive to live against the Law reap for themselves the results of a bitter harvest. Those who live with the Law reap a harvest of happiness and plenty, in the things of matter and in the things of the spirit.

Through all the darkness that prevails, do not abandon hope, but be assured in the knowledge that those who work with you for the upliftment of humankind, who strive to bring better conditions into your world of matter, will prevail, for the power that is on their side is the mightiest power in the universe.

You will not achieve that which is worth achieving without travail, without sorrow. Your world must learn its lessons in the only way it can learn them. We are breaking through all over the world of matter. Our message illumines minds in every part of your world, and, as the light of the spirit breaks in on your world, so its rays disperse the darkness of your materialism.

We do not seek to terrify you with threats of punishment. We do not seek to make you craven cowards, living your lives because of fear. We strive to make you realize the latent divinity that is yours, that you may express more of the Great Spirit, that you may rise to greater heights and fill your mind with greater truth and wisdom.

We urge you to be dissatisfied with what you have already received, because only through discontent and the desire to reach out can greater knowledge come. He who is satisfied stagnates: he who is discontented struggles towards greater freedom.

We never say to you: "Do not use your reason: have faith only." We say: "Use that which the Great Spirit has given you. Test us. Examine us. If aught that we say is debasing, cruel or immoral, then reject us."

If we seek always to teach you to live nobler lives, lives of greater self-sacrifice and of idealism, then surely that demonstrates that the hall-mark of the Great Spirit is stamped upon our teaching.

If we raise up one soul, if we give comfort to one who mourns, if we give hope to one who is faint-hearted, if we give strength to one who is weary, then has it not been worth doing?

Think of the many whom our message disturbs, whom it puzzles, who are perplexed, who, bound to a creed, cannot escape—yet they hear the voice of freedom calling to their imprisoned souls and their minds struggle to be free.

They are the ones for whom the message is intended, those to whom it comes as an incentive to reach out to what before was unattainable. All truth is but a stepping stone.

If you hear through the lips of the medium through whom I address you that which makes your reason revolt, that which contradicts the love of the Great Spirit, that which is foolish, that which is an insult to your intelligence, then know that my day is done and I have failed.

Though I have spoken to you many, many times, I do not think I have ever said anything which is contrary to the highest aspirations of the soul. For our appeal is always to the highest that is within you.

The world must learn to perform its own salvation. There is no ready-made plan. There is no prepared, cut-and-dried system. Your world has to learn that, behind what it regards as the manifestations of life, there is the eternal reality of the spirit, that the children of matter are not only worldly beings but spiritual beings expressing themselves through bodies of matter.

The bodies of matter must be as perfect as they can be made through having all the necessities of life freely at their disposal, as the Great Spirit would have them. Then their spirits must be freed from all dogmatic and creedal trammels, so that they do not give allegiance to things that have no real or spiritual value, so that they work only for that which is true, so that the warring and the quarrelling and the strife over creeds and dogmas, which have held your world in chains for thousands of years, can be abolished.

We preach the gospel of the spiritual brotherhood of all peoples, with the Great White Spirit as the common Father. What stands in the way is the earthly conception, the churches built on error, the usurping of privilege, the pride and the power of tyrants, petty tyrants who hold the whip hand.

As our teaching grows in your world, it will mean the end of all separateness between peoples. It will mean the end of national barriers. It will mean the end of race distinctions, class distinctions, colour distinctions and all the distinctions between churches and chapels, temples, mosques and synagogues, for gradually all will learn that they have a part of the Great Spirit's truth and that the part enshrined in the heart of every other religion in no way contradicts that portion which is precious to them.

So, out of the apparent confusion, the divine pattern will take its shape and harmony and peace will come. I tell you these things, so that you can understand part of the great Plan, the part that we who return from the world of spirit play in it, and the part that each one of you must play in it before your earthly course is run.

What we preach fits in with all the noble and elevated ideas that have come to the vision of all the reformers, all the saints, all the seers and all the idealists who have striven in every age to render service. Because they were great souls, their spiritual eyes caught glimpses of the life that could be, and that vision of beauty sustained them in all their adversity and struggle. They realized the spirit plan that, one day, will be put into practice, and so they strove to raise up the children of matter, to serve.

Though they were vilified, though they were opposed and ridiculed by those they came to help, their work lived on, even as the work that is being done today in countless small temples, such as this, will live on, though many of the people will be forgotten. The mighty power of the spirit has been launched once again in your world of matter, and the children of matter do not possess the power to stem that mighty tide.

Your world thinks it solves its problems by the shedding of

blood. But no problem was ever solved in that way, for bloodshed is needless and leads nowhere. Why cannot they use the reason which the Great Spirit has given them? Why do they think that their only solution must be to kill as many as possible, that the one who is the greatest killer is accounted the victor? It is a strange world you live in.

Your world needs our message, the message of the spirit, the realization of spirit truths, the knowledge that there are spiritual laws and guidance both from above and from within, so that in its perplexity it may learn where to turn to find comfort and guidance and help.

We seek nothing for ourselves. We want no glory. We have simply the desire to be of service, to reveal once again the laws which have been forgotten, so that the world of matter may rediscover those powers of the spirit which can bring it new hope and new life.

In your perplexity, when all the old standards are being discarded, when all authorities are being questioned and their power waning, we seek to reveal the Great Spirit, the supreme Authority, through His laws which never fail and which never err. If the world of matter will learn to order its life in accordance with those laws, peace and concord will rule once again.

These things are part of the great mission which we all have to perform so that, amidst the crumbling ruins of the discarded beliefs, mankind may not reject all because of his doubt and scepticism, but may learn to sift the wheat from the chaff, the fact from the myth, and hold on to that which is precious, which is enshrined in all religions, the great truths of the spirit, long overlaid with the imaginations of the children of matter.

The power of the spirit—which inspired those in days gone by, which gave them vision and courage, enthusiasm and desire to serve—is available today if the children of matter will learn to look for it in the operation of those laws which are at their disposal.

The authority of Churches, of books, of creeds, all these are waning. They are gradually being discarded. But the authority of spiritual truths abides for ever. When I return to your world I see the confusion and the chaos, and I realize they could be dissipated if the clear light of the spirit were allowed to penetrate, if, instead of just a chink, there could be a strong illuminating ray.

Why do they prefer the darkness when they could have the light? Why do they prefer ignorance when they could have knowledge? Why do they prefer superstition when they could have wisdom? Why do they prefer the dead bones of a creed when they could have the living truth of the spirit? Why do they prefer the dust of theology when they could have the waters of spiritual wisdom?

There are souls blindly groping in self-imposed darkness, chained when they could be free, servile when they could easily be men of freedom. But I am afraid they have worn their chains for so long that they are afraid to discard them. A bird that is in a cage for a long time is afraid that it cannot fly when it is released.

It is good when they throw off their shackles, but they must have some path which they can tread. We do not want them to be helpless, without a sign. We want them to be free, but we want them to know where their freedom will lead.

When you have been in bondage for a long time, there is a tendency in the newly-found freedom that you will not listen to any guidance that comes to you. You say: "I have had enough of all this. I have had years of doubt and perplexity. Now that I have discarded it I do not any longer wish to be associated with what is called religion."

Sometimes, with the casting off of shackles, there is a violent reaction. I do not want too much attention paid to me, the individual, the messenger. I am only concerned with the message.

Your world has for too long concerned itself with teachers, whom it has aggrandized into exaggerated positions, and has forgotten what they came to teach.

Our mission no longer is to exalt men and women into high places of authority, but to seek to reveal truth, knowledge and wisdom. What does it matter whether I am a teacher of great distinction or a lowly beggar, so long as the seal of truth stamps what I say? Our appeal is no longer to names and authorities and books, but to reason alone.

We demand nothing that is contrary to your intelligence. We preach nothing that you can say is untrue, that is undignified, that is ignoble, that debases mankind. We seek to reveal that which will elevate the whole human race and give it a true conception of its position in life and in the universe, its relationship to the Great White Spirit and an understanding of its kinship with other members of the vast human family in your world.

No longer will we resort to books or teachers or authorities, but only to divine Reason, and we appeal to her. Our truth will not be spread by the citation of a text said to be stamped with divine authority. If it violates reason, then reject what we say.

But you will find that we appeal to the highest and the best instincts, that we only seek to brush away old falsehoods and to bring the great truth that man will prize. What your world calls religion must be founded on truth, and you must seek to discard all that will not stand the onslaught of reason.

I am only an instrument, striving to reveal those truths which your world has had so many times and then lost, and which we are now determined shall be placed in the forefront of your world of matter, never to be lost again.

This time, we are striving to be certain that the forces of

materialism and selfishness shall not prevail, so that your world may learn to save itself from the evil which is ready to overtake it. Only the application of these truths in their ramifications in your daily lives can avert the fearful catastrophe that looms in front of you.

Your world is bankrupt and chaotic. It is filled with despair and strife and bitterness. Reason has been dethroned and selfishness rules in the world. We seek to restore reason, to replace error with truth, superstition with knowledge, darkness with light, so that those who are weak in the struggle may find strength and those who are helpless may become whole again, so that those who are tired may become refreshed, so that those who suffer injustice may have their due.

We strive to reveal these truths, not only as they are known in their relation to the laws of the spirit, but also to the laws of matter, for to us the world of matter is part of the universe of the Great Spirit, and you cannot be "religious" if you are indifferent to the sufferings of despairing humanity. Those who serve are accounted as the great ones by us, and the service they render is not confined to helping the soul to find truth, for there is other service to be rendered.

There is the service of freeing poor, racked bodies from pain, the service of fighting injustice and tyranny, the service of fighting hate, the service of preserving freedom and the service of abolishing the evils of your world and giving the spirit in man a chance to express itself as the Great Spirit desires that it should.

I am sorry that the children of the Great Spirit have wandered so far from the things of the spirit that a rap on a table has to be used to make them understand His laws.

You are all parts of the Great Spirit. He says to you: "Here are all My laws and here, in you, is a part of Me. Beside you there is all that can be used to make a perfect universe. I give you all the tools and you can choose between the things that are right and the things that are wrong. You can try to work with My laws or against them."

The children have chosen. But always those who are the masters in the world of spirit have to make sure that they incarnate into matter men who are so tuned to the vibrations of the Great Spirit that, through them, His work can go on. So far have the children wandered that they are blind to the things of the spirit and only understand the things of matter.

But after the storms and the wind have blown through the world there always comes the new life of the Spring. When the snow lies on the ground and all looks very bleak, you are not able to see the freshness of the Spring. But it comes.

And gradually, as the great sun of life moves through the heavens of the Great Spirit, so the majesty of life comes to its fullest. Throughout the whole world of matter there is a great cloud of discontent. There will come the Spring of dreams and the Summer of fulfilment.

It will come quickly or slowly as the children of the Great Spirit exercise their free will. But wherever in the world of matter one man strives to uplift one other man, then behind him there are a thousand spirits who try to make his victory a greater one. No effort for good can ever be lost. No desire to serve can ever be wasted.

There must be a pioneer who hacks his way through the forest and makes the path a little easier for those who follow. Gradually the path is beaten down and worn smooth.

Sometimes I see the many masters in my world, with tears in their eyes, looking down on the follies of those who, one day, will realize how they have thrown away the great opportunities they had of raising up the children of the earth. And sometimes I see their faces wreathed in smiles because, in your world, some unknown man has rendered a service which lights a new torch of hope in the world.

I, like many others, have come nearer to the vibrations of

the earth to help to push forward that great new world which waits just round the corner. I come to teach you the laws of the Great Spirit, and to show you how, if you live according to them, the bounty of the Great Spirit can be poured into your hearts and minds.

I only see a world filled with sorrow that should be filled with happiness, darkness where there should be light, hunger where there should be plenty. I see that the Great Spirit has provided everything, and yet there are those who are preventing its distribution. There are obstacles which must be swept away.

I cannot do it. I cannot even criticize. I can only tell you how the Law can work if you, who are still encased in matter, will allow it to work through you. Those who do must point a finger of scorn to the things of earth and show the remedies of the Great Spirit.

Show in your own lives you know the things of the spirit because the power of the spirit is in you. If I can teach you the laws and how they work, then I rejoice. If, between us, we can in one case bring happiness where there was unhappiness, knowledge where there was ignorance, then at least we shall have done some service. We do not seek to take away from you the responsibilities of your own lives, but only to try to inspire you to live so that men may know the Great Spirit is working through you.

It makes me sad, sometimes, to hear people say: "Oh yes, we give them bread, but they must thank the Great Spirit first." Why not give the bread and not worry whether they thank the Great Spirit or not? If a man is hungry, why not give him bread? Or they say: "You can sleep here, but you must say a prayer."

Have you who possess this knowledge of Spiritualism ever tried to strike a balance? You have something that your world cannot measure. You have the priceless knowledge of the truths of the Great Spirit. You have the realization that your soul is linked with His great soul. You have the knowledge that you are a part of the Great Spirit. You have learned how to respond to the vibrations of the messengers that the Great Spirit sends to watch over you.

Compared with these things, the things of matter are as mere baubles. You will live for many thousands of years. You will find that the knowledge you have gained here and the wisdom you have learned are of greater value to the life of your immortal soul than the few things that the body of matters seeks in the world of matter.

Do not judge anything by the apparent result. You see only with the eyes of matter. If you could see with the eyes of the spirit, you would know that with every child there is perfect justice. Sometimes I listen to your prayers and sometimes to the prayers of others. I think that if the Great Spirit were to answer them all you would not be happy with the result.

I have spoken to many who have crossed from your world to mine. I have not yet met one who has said, when he saw with the eyes of the spirit, that he has not been served well by the Great Spirit.

There are three great problems in the world of matter. One is ignorance, another is sorrow, and the third is poverty. These three things you will always have until knowledge of the spirit is joined with politics and the children of earth think and live as the New Knowledge shows them.

But the tide of victory rolls on. The old order dies, giving place to the new. The New World is coming. But do not think that, because of this victory, there will be no more dark places. There will still be much shedding of tears. There will be many aching hearts. There is great sacrifice to be made.

That which is a part of the Great Spirit cannot be achieved without sacrifice. You cannot build up unless you tear down. In times of great material disaster, the people of your world begin to examine the foundations of the things of the spirit. When all the things of matter have failed, they look for a reed to clutch, and they look into the systems that have been tried and found wanting.

Then the truths of the spirit begin to emerge, and they begin to build their new world—a world where the laws of the Great Spirit begin to play their proper part. Until you do that, there will always be great troubles. The world will never become perfect, because the nearer perfection it becomes, the more will it realize the perfection in front of it.

* * * * *

Questions and Answers:

If the spirit world is interested in propaganda for Spiritualism why has it not made greater effort in regard to newspaper inquiries?

Oh, how little you know. It is always good that knowledge is spread. Who are you to judge the value of propaganda? You do not always know when souls are touched.

We have our own methods. Our plans are all prepared, we only need the co-operation of your world to help us.

But you must always remember we do not wave a wand. We offer no magical formulæ. We seek to reveal the natural laws of the universe.

We seek to touch the souls of your people so that they can understand that they are all parts of the Great Spirit and the laws of the Great Spirit can work through them. Our propaganda never ceases. It is not always done by the noise of your world, but by impressing the soul and the heart, by closer union with the spirit.

Are not the experiences on this earth—such as war, pain, mental and physical suffering, disease, sorrow, love, hate, joy and happiness—essential for the development and progress of mankind and a part of the divine plan?

No, they are not. Wars are not made by the Great Spirit. Disease is not given by the Great Spirit. These are the things that the children of matter have brought upon themselves by the misuse of their free will. There are lessons to be learned, but they can be learned without the brutalities and the hideous cruelties that the children of the Great Spirit perpetrate against each other. Do not mistake the doings of man for the acts of the Great Spirit.

Do you consider the maintenance of the "British Empire," now a commonwealth, to be advantageous to the world?

Yes, because all that which binds people in unity is to be prized. The world must learn to draw closer together, seeking to find those factors of unity on which it can stand together.

That is why we are opposed to those who strive for separation. When the soul is liberated it desires to draw together in harmony all the others in the world.

Why is it that we hear so much about a spirit plan, and yet see such little apparent result of it?

You do not see the results of a plan because you look at these things with the eyes of matter. You judge progress in relation to your own short span of life, but we see progress because we look at things from another plane. We see the spread of knowledge, a greater understanding of spiritual things, a rise of tolerance, an increase of good will, a breaking down of barriers of ignorance and superstition and fear and spiritual slavery.

It is not as if there were to be a sudden revolution. That could never happen, because all spiritual growth must be slow and progressive. Do not think that there is need for despair. There is on one hand—when you see the growing masses of materialistic forces—but on the other hand there is growing hope as the light of spiritual truth penetrates the fog of materialistic selfishness. And, as long as knowledge spreads, truth will be victorious.

That is why our message is so important. It is not for us—it is for you. It is we who strive to serve you, to make your world realize the price it must pay for its selfishness, for its wanton ignorance, its deliberate cruelty. We strive to serve you, to help you, because we love you.

We are not evil spirits, seeking to lure you on to paths of destruction. We do not seek to make you debase yourselves, to practise cruelty or sin. Rather do we strive to make you realize the divinity that is yours, the powers of the Great Spirit that you possess, how you can practise the law of service and help the Plan of the Great Spirit.

THE WORLD OF TOMORROW

What will be the world of the future, when man has learned the laws of the spirit and lives according to their dictates? The birth of this New World cannot be ordained by any dictator or government or league of nations. It will come only when men have earned it. A taste of the joys to come is given by Silver Birch below:

YOU are now in the midst of the crisis. As always happens before there is a birth, there is much pain. The birth of the new order means much pain. Even when the new order comes, there will be growing pains.

But there has been planted in your world a seed that will grow, and the efforts of those in high places to destroy the seed will fail. It was said, a long time ago: "Thy will be done on earth as it is in Heaven." That is going to happen.

There will be many big changes. There will be break-ups, and there will be many upheavals. There will be what you think is darkness and difficulty. You will say "Things are worse." But, all the time, there is behind it all a power which is making for the progress of the world.

There are many of us who have been allowed by those who are higher and above us to see your world as it will be one day. That conception we try to transmit to those who are receptive, to inspire them to go on with their work. The pictures I have seen make your present world more ugly than it is. I see what it could be like—and what it must be like. It is only a question of time.

One day, there will arise a new race that will recognize that all politics, religion, science and knowledge are part of one thing. Then pain, sorrow, fear, mourning and unhappiness will be banished and your world will be a place of smiles and happy laughter. The greatest teacher who could come into your world today would be one who could work to lift the sorrows of others and make the lives of others better.

You have tried to build a world where, when one man has something, instead of using it to help the others, he tries to keep it for himself, with the result that in time he makes a system that must collapse because its foundations are wrong.

When you have people who develop their gifts, which all come from the Great Spirit, and use them for the benefit of all the others, then there will be built a system founded on that which is eternal.

They are not new things that we try to teach you. They are the old, old truths that those who have seen with the eyes of the spirit have taught you for many, many years. But you have neglected them and so it is necessary for us to teach them to you once again, to show you that you must learn the lessons of the Great Spirit. You have nearly destroyed your world by the follies of your own ideas.

Your world must get back to the Great Spirit and His laws. It is coming back. Slowly, I can see how the laws of the Great Spirit are coming into fulfilment.

What you must try to learn is that the bounty of the Great Spirit must be properly divided amongst the people. You have people who have too little to eat and you have people with too much to eat. That, of course, must be wrong. You have to divide the things you have among the people that you have. Is not that simple?

You must break down vested interests. The laws are perfect. If you live your own life, seeking only to serve others, then because of that the Great Spirit operates through you. That applies to you and it applies to all. If you say it is not possible, I say it is possible, for it is the only way. The Law is perfect and you cannot cheat it. You must learn the Law and put it into operation.

For many, many years the children of earth have used their free will to build up that which has to be destroyed. Slowly, the light of the Great White Spirit has been penetrating the darkness of your world, and out of the ruins of its chaos and disorder there is being built a new world of the Great Spirit, where there will be no inequality, no injustice, no division of those who have too much from those who have too little, where all the gifts will be divided and all the bounty will be evenly spread.

I do not care by what name you call the dawn of the new world, but it is the world of the Great Spirit coming into fulfilment, accompanied by His power, and the service of all faithful hearts who seek but to bring new joy, new life, new happiness into the world of matter, so that there shall cease coming into our world the wrecks of yours.

Sometimes you may think that that work is being retarded, but all the time there is being used, even against their knowledge, people in all places, instruments unknown even to themselves. The Great Spirit will not allow His children to destroy themselves. That is why I have urged you again and again to help. Whether you call it politics or not, I do not care. The work goes on. We all work together. It cannot be stopped now.

I am proud that because of our efforts we have accomplished so much throughout the world of matter. Hearts that were once sad are now a little more joyful. Light has pierced the gloom of darkness. Now, there is a little more knowledge where before there was ignorance. We have aided those who have become faint-hearted, given strength to those who were weary, guided those who had lost their way and acted as an incentive to those who strive to work for their fellows, giving them the realization that behind them there is a mighty host of spirit spurring them on in all their endeavours for the Great Spirit and His children.

And I am also happy that I have been able to bring to you some of those you love and who love you, so that you may realize more than you ever did before that you have never lost them, that death does not divide but brings together those whom love and affection and friendship have made one in heart and soul.

I wish you could see the extent of our influence. We have helped to break barriers, to remove obstacles and to bring knowledge. These are the things your world needs, the simple truths that will enable spiritual, mental and material freedom to come to your world. As you know, we live only to serve, for through service and service alone can your world be saved from itself.

I want to remind you all once again I am only an instrument. I am only one of many seeking to bring you the truth, the simple truth of the spirit, the realization that you are all parts of the Great Spirit of all life. The Great Spirit is within you. You have a divine heritage and are entitled to all the bounty of the Great Spirit because of your latent divinity, and all obstacles and institutions that stand in the way of that fullness must be swept aside. Our labour is not only to free the souls and minds, but the bodies also.

That is the task to which we have dedicated ourselves. That is the service we strive to perform. If I, as an instrument, am privileged to bring you those truths which help you, then I rejoice. I have worked among you for some time and I will continue to work with you, so that through our united efforts we may bring some help—help that is badly needed—into your world. You have the knowledge, you have the truth, you have the responsibility that comes with all knowledge ot using it so that you are greater instruments.

Remember always, when men question you, that the hall-mark of divine truth is stamped on our message because we appeal only to your reason. The message that we bring you is one that does not debase you, that does not demean your intelligence, that does not seek to turn you from the paths of service, goodness or rectitude. Rather does it strive to make you realize your latent divinity, so that, conscious of your own tie with the Great Spirit, you may so order your lives that the Great Spirit of all life is expressed in all that you do.

Great work can be achieved if all those who are conscious of spiritual truths will band themselves together and use their power to dissipate the fog of darkness which has risen in the world of matter. Go forward with great confidence, knowing that all the forces of goodness, helpfulness and service are at your side.

There is a great field for service in front of us all. We look forward with joyful anticipation to the fact that we will be able to help many who do not know where to turn, who have left behind them the old shibboleths, who do not trust any more the faith of yesterday and who search for the truth which will withstand the questionings of today. We bring them the knowledge of spiritual truth and spiritual law. We seek to remind them of their own innate powers of divinity, to make them understand the Godhood that is theirs, so that they may sweep away for ever the ideas of cringing self-abasement before a vengeful, wrathful deity.

We seek to make your world of matter realize the great power of spirit, waiting to co-operate with all those who strive to serve the children of the Great Spirit, so that, armed with knowledge, they can fight all superstition and all that belongs to the mists of darkness, and allow the light of spiritual truth to radiate its glorious beams. That is our task. And we bring with us that power of the spirit which can inspire and guide, which can uphold and sustain, which can bring food to hungry minds, healing to bodies racked with pain, which can bring inspiration and revelation, truth and wisdom for all.

We can fill them with this power just as they provide us with the capacity to understand and receive it. We seek to co-operate with all who desire to uplift mankind, whether they be inside the Churches or outside, whether they have the labels of religion or none at all, whether they be scientists, materialists, philosophers.

ALL IS RULED BY LAW

The universe is governed by natural laws which cannot be set aside. No guide can alter these laws or enable anyone to escape the consequences of breaking them, but he can explain them and thus help to remove the danger of ignorance. Some of these laws, just as real as the law of gravity, for instance, are explained here by Silver Birch:

WE try to teach the laws of the Great Spirit, which would enable health and happiness to be in your world of matter. All those who speak in your churches must one day undo all the wrong they have done. They do not escape the Law. None escapes the Law; particularly, all who have heard the voice of the spirit. If they fail, it is worse for them than for those who have not heard.

When your eyes are opened and your hearts have received the love that comes with the power of the spirit, when your minds have had the revelations of spirit truths, if, after that, you fail in service, the greater is the punishment that comes to you, for you have done it with knowledge and not in ignorance. There are many mediums who could be instruments who have sold their gifts for thirty pieces of silver.

The Great Spirit is within you all and, though you have risen and ascended through all forms of evolution and there is within each one of you a trace of your animal ancestry, which is part of your heredity, greater than all those things are the powers of the Great Spirit within you which, if you would but allow them to function and to express themselves, would enable you to walk the earth like gods.

Your world does not realize that each individual contains

within his own being the power to conquer every disease, to master every difficulty. He possesses a reservoir of strength from which he can draw in moments of weakness. The kingdom of heaven is within. How little is that understood!

The way to contact that higher self is by living one's life in accordance with the laws of the Great Spirit. But how many do it?

Life consists not only of the things you do, but of the things you say and the things you think. Do not imagine that only your deeds count. They do to a large extent, but your words and your thoughts are also part of you. It is sad that so many of you are slaves to your thoughts, instead of being their masters.

The guide has often spoken on the need for universal brotherhood:

WE are all parts of the Great White Spirit. Some He has painted red, some black, some yellow, and some He has not painted at all, but all these colours are part of His scheme.

Some day His laws will come into your world, and harmony will come when the colours mix together and live together with love in their hearts. You do not understand what these colours mean. Each has a great purpose and contributes to the laws of life.

There will not be any peace in your world until all these colours blend together, until men learn not to look at the skins, but at the souls that are behind them.

Has it ever occurred to you that you have in this circle, in the guides and the sitters, a commonwealth of nearly all the nations? That is a great lesson for your world.

We have learned how the people of other races can bring

into the pool that which is special to them. Out of that comes what is best for the whole. Your world does not understand yet that the man who has a yellow skin has something which can help the rest of the world, and the white man also has something distinctive which would be of assistance to the others.

You must remember that each one of you is a part of the Great Spirit. Each one of you can add to His work, His power, His love and His knowledge. Even as you try to lift up all those who are less strong than yourselves, so the power of the Great Spirit is able to manifest through you.

It does not matter which way you do it, or who you help, or where you bring light into darkness, so long as you raise up those who have fallen down, give strength to those who are weak, bring light where there is darkness, give food to those who are hungry and sleep to those who have nowhere to lay their heads.

That is all a part of the work of the Great Spirit. Wherever you make that effort there will always come to you more power to sustain, inspire and uplift you, so that you will be able to do more even than you understand.

The Great Spirit moves many people, not always within churches or cathedrals or temples, but where there are instruments who can respond to the power of the spirit, who can be moved by His power and who can uplift because they are fired with a zeal from on high, from the Highest of the High.

Your world thinks that the power of the Great Spirit can be limited and made to flow in the channels which it thinks ought to be used, but the Great Spirit uses those channels where His inspiration can pour down into your world of matter, wherever hearts are attuned to Him, wherever minds are accessible to Him, and wherever human spirits are in tune with Him.

That power of the spirit ignores all earthly distinctions and cares not for rank or title, grade of society, colour, race, nationality or class. It recognizes only those who can respond, wherever they may be, whoever they may be, and fills them with the power which cometh from the Source of all Truth, illumines their minds, stimulates their souls and makes them workers in the great vineyard.

May you all learn that lesson and, filled with determination to work for the Great Spirit and for those of His children who suffer in darkness, in stress and storm, in trouble, may you lighten their load and bring to them a new hope, a new knowledge, a new light, a new strength, so that, their bodies filled with new power, their minds with courage and their spirits refreshed, they may be able to enjoy the bounty of the Great Spirit. You will learn the joy of service, a service that asks nothing for itself but only to uplift others.

Silver Birch has told of a "great secret" that has not yet been learned in the material world:

THE Great Spirit is infinite, and you are parts of the Great Spirit. If you have perfect faith and live your lives right, then you are able to participate in the bounty of the Great Spirit.

If every person in your world had perfect faith, then he would receive. If a person were hungry and yet had perfect faith, then he would receive the answer.

That is how the Law operates. If you learn to attune yourselves to the Law, the results must come. If the results do not come, that only proves that you are not in tune with the Law. Your history books tell you that there have been those from the lowest of the low, the poorest of the poor, who have tried the Law—and it has not failed them. You must not point to those who do not try it and ask why it does not work.

Sometimes the spirit gets crushed and cannot rise above the

surrounding circumstances, but if you had perfect faith you could rise above all the troubles of your world. You would turn your faces to the sun, which is but an emblem of the Great Spirit, and say: "I am a part of the Great Spirit. I am indestructible. I am eternal. I am infinite. That which is finite and part of the world of matter cannot touch me." If you did that, you would not be touched.

Many people start with fear in their hearts. They are afraid they will not get results, and the element of fear disturbs the vibration. Perfect love casteth out fear! Seek ye first the kingdom of God and His righteousness, and all these things shall be added unto you!

That was taught to you many years ago by one who knew the Law. He showed that when he put it into operation the results were always forthcoming. If you allow the Law to function, then the results must come.

I will tell you another Law. There is nothing you can have in the world of matter without you pay the price. The price of mediumship is increased sensitiveness. You cannot accumulate wealth without paying the price because if you do that, and forget the duties of your own spirit, then you may be rich in the goods of your world, but you will be very poor in my world.

You have the greatest riches within yourselves. You are part of the Great Spirit. There are no riches or fortunes in your world that can be compared with that. We seek to teach you to explore your own gold mines, to reveal the diamonds of the spirit that are within the clay of your own natures.

May you all learn to respond to vibrations of the highest planes of spirit. May you all realize that you are never alone, but always encompassed around and about by a host of those who love you, who seek to guard and guide you and to help and inspire you. And may you, as you unfold your own spirits, realize that you are being drawn closer to the greatest Spirit of all, becoming more in unison with His Law.

You serve Him by serving the children of matter. When you do that, you are within reach of His infinite arms, you are surrounded by His love, which will bring you to perfect peace.

Faith that is faith alone sometimes fails when the winds of bitter experience blow. But the faith that is born of knowledge provides a foundation which is so strong that no wind of circumstance can disturb it.

Blessed are those who believe and have not yet seen, but thrice blessed are they who know and, because they know, place their faith in that which is not yet revealed to them, because they know that the laws of the universe are operated by a power which is love and wisdom.

You should all have perfect faith, because it is a faith born of knowledge. You have had the proof of the power of the Spirit. Now you should have the faith that all things work wisely and well and that, if you put yourselves in tune with the laws of the Great Spirit, then you must reap the operation of those laws.

You can all banish from your minds the thought that anything that is unenlightened—or, as you would say, evil—can ever touch you. You live and move under the protection of the Great Spirit and His laws.

If there is no evil in your hearts, then only good can reach you, for only good can dwell where goodness reigns. None but the servants of the Great Spirit come into your presence from my world. You need have no fears. The power which envelops you, the power which supports and seeks to guide you and inspire you, is the power that emanates from the Great Spirit of all.

That power can sustain you in all your trials and difficulties. That power can change your storms into sunshine, and bring you out of the darkness of despair into the light of knowledge.

Your feet are set on pathways of progress. There is no need for fear.

Perfect love casteth out fear. Knowledge dispels fear, for fear is born of ignorance. Where there is love and trust and knowledge, there fear cannot reign. An evolved spirit cannot be afraid at any time, because he knows there is no experience that can come to him in any phase of life that he cannot master, for he is the Great Spirit.

Fear creates its own prison for the soul. You must learn to rise above fear and not to allow its vibrations to hinder you, to have perfect faith and confidence and trust, to know that you can stand on your feet and say: "I am the Great Spirit and the wind of circumstance cannot shake me. I will rise triumphant over every difficulty because of the infinite power which is within my soul." You have power over every circumstance. Would you limit the power of the infinite soul?

The Great Spirit rules over that which is material and that which is spiritual. There are no divisions in His universal kingdom. Do not attempt to divide the life of matter from the life of spirit. They are not distinct and separate. They are parts of one indivisible life, for the things of matter react on the things of spirit and the things of spirit react on the things of matter.

You have yet to learn that there are no difficulties which beset those blessed with the power of the spirit that they will not surmount, as long as they in return serve the Great White Spirit wherever they go.

There are no obstacles in your world we cannot remove, if it is the law that they shall be removed. If, sometimes, the cross you have seems very hard to bear, remember that, although I would give up all my progress to take it away from you, it is better for you to carry it and to learn the lesson it brings. You must consider not only this life, but the whole of eternity.

If you children of matter would but remember that not only are you human, but also divine, how much easier would it be for you to live your lives.

Your troubles would melt away, your obstacles would be swept on one side. But you have little faith in the power that is within you. What you call human belongs to the world of matter. That which is divine belongs to the Great Spirit.

Many years ago you were told to be in the world, but not of the world. Because the people of your world have not the faith, then the Law cannot be put into operation. You say one has more money and less worry than another. You do not know how their worries compare. The laws of the Great Spirit cannot be cheated.

You are on earth to build your characters. It is the way you face your problems that makes your character. But there is no trouble in your world of matter which is greater than the power you have within you for overcoming it, because the troubles are of the earth, material, and you are part of the Great Spirit, divine.

There is only one peace—the peace which comes to those who are at one with the Great Spirit, whose hearts beat as one with His great heart, whose wills are at one with His great will, who are at one in soul, mind and heart with the Great Spirit. Then there is peace, because they are in harmony with His laws. There is no other peace.

I can only teach you the laws. You were told many years ago that the kingdom of heaven is within. It is not without. It is not to be found in the rush of the world of matter. It is to be found within the soul.

So finely balanced and so perfect is the Law that there can be no cheating. Not one person escapes his punishment, and not one loses his reward. Do not judge eternity with the eyes of matter. Do not judge the smaller when you have not seen the greater.

Do not confuse the transient joys of earth with the enduring things of the spirit. They are tawdry and flimsy. You think in terms of the earth, while I see with the eyes of the spirit. I cannot alter the Law to please you.

If you ask all those who return to you from my side, you will find that they all say the Law is perfect. They never want to return to the world of matter. You seek to find peace without. I try to show you the eternal peace within. The greatest riches are the riches of the spirit.

Some people will always worry. Even in the world of spirit they will worry. They will worry because they will realize they could be more perfect, because they are not perfect instruments for the Great Spirit, because only through toil and stress will they outwork the imperfections of their natures and allow the divine to shine through.

Do you think we are happy when we realize the work that has yet to be done? Do you think we do not worry when we see the children of matter denied that which is necessary for their sustenance, or when we hear the false teaching that is poured out in the name of the Great Spirit?

Do you think we do not worry when we see darkness where there should be light, when men are imprisoned by desire when they could be free, when we see the chaos that has been caused in your world?

We worry because our hearts are filled with pity, because we seek to enable the love of the Great Spirit to flow through us and you into your world of matter, where so many are denied the things that are their heritage. The Great Spirit has given them all things in abundance, but they are denied them. You cannot be a great soul when others starve and you are filled with plenty.

The hardest part of our task is when we have to stand by, sometimes, and see you suffer. We know we must not help because it is a battle of your own spirit. If you win your battle, then we have won, too. If you lose, then we have lost. It is our battle all the time, but we must not lift a finger to help.

Sometimes I have wept tears because I have seen suffering, and knew I must not help. That is the Law. It has hurt me more than it has hurt the sufferer.

If you do what you know is right, then you cannot do any more. If that means that sometimes you must deny yourself, then you must do it. One day a balance is struck.

I cannot solve your problems for you. If I tell you what to do, that interferes with your free will. Once I start to tell my medium what he must do and what he must not do, that is the end of his free will. Then his progress begins to suffer.

It is the way you settle your problems that develops what is within you. You do not develop the spirit when everything is easy and smooth, but when you have difficulties. But there are times when we feel justified in interfering with your judgment.

I would interfere if a very vital principle were involved. If it meant that my work through my medium would be interrupted, then I would interfere so that the channel would still be free. But where the problems only affect my medium's own evolution, then they are his responsibility and he must work them out for himself.

Silver Birch has spoken of the great responsibility of those who use their free will in order to deny others the things which are their heritage:

THOSE who stand between the children of earth and all those things which sustain their bodies and their spirit, have a very big responsibility. One day, either in your world or in mine, they will have to pay the price.

Sometimes I get very tired with those who want what they call "higher teachings" from the spirit world and do nothing to help their brother men. As people grow, they understand more and more the operation of the laws of the Great Spirit. There is no "high" and there is no "low" teaching.

If all the people who clamour for teachings would do something to make the earth a better place, a brighter place, a place where the hungry would be fed and the thirsty would be given drink, where people were allowed to live in houses where the sunshine of the Great Spirit could reach their poor, tired bodies, then they would be putting into operation the highest teaching of all.

Stressing that most of our troubles are brought about by the exercise of our own free will, Silver Birch once said:

IF you are faced with a war, there will be many who will say: "Why doesn't the Great Spirit stop it? Why doesn't the Great Spirit prevent it?" Yet, all the time, the people of your world are to blame if they choose to ignore His laws.

Do not think that your world can escape the consequences of its actions. We cannot alter the Law. What has been sown must be reaped. You have sown selfishness; you must reap the results. Pride, jealousy, envy, greed, malice, distrust, suspicion—all these things, when they fructify, produce war, distress, discord.

We who strive to express the Law of the Great Spirit are often criticized by those who do not understand the purpose which is behind our coming to your world. But we only seek to reveal the Law, for there is nothing else in your world, whether you call it religion, or science, or philosophy, but the natural law of the Great Spirit.

Whoever it is, whether it be the one or the many, the race

or the nation, that seek to live against the Law, they must pay the price. I have always told you that the Law is perfect in its operation. Sometimes you do not see the fulfilment, but I know that cause and effect always follow each other, because it is the Law. I have always told you these things. That is why I tell you again that there is nothing but the Law—the Law of the Great Spirit.

We seek to reveal the Great Spirit, but we can only reveal Him through His laws. We seek to teach you the Law, so that you may live your lives in harmony with that Law. Yours is the free will to choose. Whether it is the free will of the one or the many it is the same.

Until your world learns that it must plan with the Law and not against it, there will be chaos, bankruptcy, disaster and ruin everywhere. We can do nothing but teach you the eternal principles of the spirit, because they are the enduring things that remain long after that which is material decays and crumbles into the dust. Man, whose eyes are cast only on the things of matter, makes a great mistake, because he chases illusion and forgets eternity. These are the simple truths, but your world has not yet learned them.

But through bitter travail and tears, through bloodshed and sorrow, they must learn them, if they will not learn them any other way. I would rather that you learn them as we seek to express them, in all love, in all desire of service to one another. But if you will not learn through the ways of the spirit, then you must pay the price for attempting to live against the Law. The great ones of your world are not the great ones of my world. We see greatness as greatness of soul, greatness of spirit, greatness in desire to serve. These things will endure long after the glitter of the material world has disappeared.

Free will is a gift of the Great Spirit, but if it is not used aright then the price must be paid. If the world lives with the

Law, it reaps the benefits. If it lives against the Law, it reaps the results. One way brings peace and happiness and plenty, the other way misery and war and bloodshed and chaos.

We are despised in your world of matter by those who should be the teachers of the children of the Great Spirit. We are rejected by those who should welcome us because we come in the name of the Great Spirit and His love. Filled with the desire to serve, we seek to reveal those laws and that power which will show your world how to save itself.

And those who are steeped in the ignorance of spiritual blindness, and who surround themselves with ceremony and ritual, and at the same time deny the power of the Great Spirit to descend today, must pay the price. We are the friends of all who seek to serve. We are the enemies only of those who seek to destroy. We come on wings of love and service ready to help wherever we can. That is the great task that we all have to perform.

I know that we will encounter difficulties and obstacles. But we will surmount them. The tide will ebb and flow, but it will be a winning tide. We all do so little alone, but between us we can do something. If we raise up one soul, if we bring light to one in darkness, if we bring strength to one who is weak, or comfort to one who is distressed, then we have done something.

Silver Birch was once asked whether free will was limited in the sense that there are definite tendencies of events in relation to individuals. He replied:

THERE are tendencies, vibrations, but these are not insuperable. You are surrounded by radiations and influences, much of which can affect your destiny, but the Great Spirit has provided you with part of Himself, a part of

His spirit which, when your free will is properly used according to your evolution, can enable you to conquer all that stands in the way of the fullest expression of that part of the Great Spirit that is within you. For you are the Great Spirit and the Great Spirit is you.

The seed of the Great Spirit is planted within every human soul, and, like the seed which is planted in the earth, if you give it that which makes it grow aright, then the little seed will first shoot up through the earth and gradually it will bloom until it bursts into the full beauty of the flower.

The Great Spirit has planted the seed within you, but you are the gardener and it depends on your efforts whether and when the fullness of the flower is able to express itself. There is always your free will. If you keep the seed in the darkness and do not give it the light of soul-growth, of charity, of service, then the Great Spirit is not being expressed through you.

Questioned as to the value of suffering, Silver Birch said:

EVERY experience is part of the pattern of your life. You try to judge eternity by temporal happenings. You see in matter apparent confusion, but you do not realize that a divine thread runs throughout all your lives.

In the great universe where harmony is the Law, each one of you contributes to the Plan. The events in your lives, sometimes of bitterness and despair, of pain and misery, all play their part in preparing the soul gradually for the path that is being trodden.

The darkness and the light, the shadow and the sunshine, are all but reflections of one whole. Without shadow there could be no light and without light there could be no shadow. The difficulties of life are steps which enable the soul to rise.

Difficulties, obstacles, handicaps—these are the trials of the soul. And when it conquers them all, it rises stronger, more purified, deepened in intensity and more highly evolved.

Do you think that the latent powers of the soul, infinite in their possibilities of expression, could realize themselves without difficulty and pain, without shadow, without sorrow, and without suffering and misery? Of course not.

The joy and the laughter can only be enjoyed to the full when once you have drained the cup of sorrow to the dregs, for as low as you can fall in the scale of life so correspondingly you can rise. The more you have tasted and experienced that which seems the shadow of earthly life, the more you will appreciate, because of it, the greater joys of the sunshine.

Your experiences are all part of your evolution. One day, freed from the trammels of flesh, with eyes not clouded by matter, you will look back in retrospect and view the life you have lived on earth. And out of the jigsaw of all the events, you will see how every piece fits into its allotted place, how every experience was a lesson to quicken the soul and to enable it to have greater understanding of its possibilities.

There is no experience that comes to the human soul, which, rightly understood and rightly faced, does not leave you better for it. Can you contemplate a world of matter where there were no difficulties, no trials, no troubles, no pain, no suffering? There would be no evolution. There would be nothing to surmount. You would decay.

Silver Birch has frequently talked of the sacredness of all life. Once, a sitter, on holiday, had taken part in a fox shoot, and the guide was asked whether it was wrong. The following discussion ensued:

ALL life belongs to the Great White Spirit, and no one must take it, in whatever form it is.

But the fox had eaten twenty chickens.

Suppose I gave the fox a gun and told him to shoot you because you had eaten twenty chickens! The Great White Spirit has provided for all His children, everywhere. It is man who makes them starve, not the fox.

When the children of earth have begun to evolve into higher beings, all their gross desires will fall away. When you can create the fox, or the chicken, then you can take its life away. If it is true that you can kill the chicken and the fox, then it is right for a man to kill his brother.

Life does not belong to man. It belongs to the Great White Spirit. Whenever anyone takes it away, he must answer for it some day.

What of the menace of rabbits in Australia?

You take something away from where it should be, and then you complain at the result. It was the same with the white man who came to my country. He brought those things which were good in the white man's land, but not good in the lands of the Indian.

He also brought war, "firewater", many things that helped to bring sadness to the Indian. We did not know how to shoot with firearms until the white man came and he said it was right to kill.

One day you will understand the law of the Father, which is that all things in the universe—animal, bird, fish or flower—are all parts of the Great White Spirit's plan. They are all there as parts of the creation of the Great White Spirit.

PROBLEMS OF HEALING

We are told that the healing power is latent within all of us, in the same way that we all have incipient powers of mediumship, if only we take the trouble to develop them. But while some people appear able to heal without any conscious development, the powers of others are so slight that attempts to stimulate them seem almost a waste of time. Silver Birch explains here why there is this apparent difference in our ability to heal:

YOU all have qualities of soul, and these qualities are nearer expression in some people than they are in others. As you strive for unfoldment, that quality, the psyche, the spiritual, call it what you will, unfolds and there is a closer co-operation between the instrument and the guides who work with him.

The attunement is higher, finer and closer. The rays blend into one state of beauteous harmony and, when that stage reaches its zenith, the band of workers in my world and the instrument in yours become as one in unity. The nearer you are to that state of achievement, the higher and the greater and more powerful rays that belong to our spheres can be used through the band of guides and the instrument.

(The above refers particularly to spiritual healers and not necessarily to those who practise magnetic and other forms.)

Silver Birch, discussing healing generally, once said:

WHEN you are ready to be healed, it means that the time for you to come to the spirit world is not yet, that the experience necessary for the soul through suffering of the body is over. But there are other experiences in the world of matter which the soul must have before it is ready to enter its new life. The physical suffering of the body is not the limit of human experience!

Healers are permitted to alleviate suffering because the healing enables the soul to find itself. Great as is the work of healing, there is a greater work that healers perform—they touch the souls of those who come near them and enable them to find themselves. In comparison with this, the healing of bodies is less important.

You who dwell in bodies of matter think only of lives in your world. We who have left the earth place it in its proper proportion as only a speck of your infinite lives. All your focus is wrong.

You see a poor soul suffering and, very rightly, the compassion rises in your breast. I do not condemn that. But you only think in terms of the suffering, not realizing that the time spent in that suffering is infinitesimal compared with the compensating joys.

To you, the shadows always seem longer than the sunlight—but they are not. But you must also realize that not all who are sick can be healed by healers. There are laws at work, and some people the healer cannot cure.

It is no accident that when the time is ripe the sick man is healed, just as it is no accident that when the soul is ready for its new experience beyond the gate of death the physical body drops away. It is all determined by Law. But you play your part in that Law, for you are all parts of the Great Spirit.

If all the debts were paid—and they are never paid—you would have reached the stage where pain could not touch you, for your body would be perfect. But you always contract debts, in your world and in mine.

The following conversation between Silver Birch and a sitter gives an insight into the causes of disability:

SILVER BIRCH: There is a relationship between the body of matter and the body of spirit. Man's two bodies constantly react on each other. The body of matter is dependent on the body of spirit for its existence, but the body of spirit is dependent on the body of matter for its expression in the world of matter. And it is the experiences gained through the physical body that determine the growth of the body of spirit.

SITTER: *Does the physical body conform to the pattern of the etheric?*

Yes.

Then, if a man is ill, is it the etheric body that we should treat?

That is the object of all spiritual healing. But sometimes there are conditions that have purely physical causes. That is where the skill of the medical man comes in. But anything which affects the body of matter also affects the body of spirit, and, in the same way, anything that affects the spirit reacts on the body of matter.

Then should not the etheric body always be dealt with?

Not necessarily. It depends on where the trouble begins. If it is a trouble of the spirit body, then the healing could be effected through the body of spirit. But if the trouble is caused by something that is purely physical, then it can be dealt with by physical means easier than by spiritual means.

You are a spirit now, but while you are expressing yourself through a body of matter, as well as through a body of spirit, you are dependent on the body of matter for the sensations of the world of matter. Everything that happens in your world affects your body of matter and, in turn, your body of spirit.

At the same time, everything that affects your spiritual body reacts on your physical body. There are forces of action and reaction at work all the time. There is a constant interplay of forces, physical, mental, and spiritual.

Would an illness caused by infection come through purely physical causes?

Not necessarily, because there are many diseases that have no real physical causes, but start with the spirit.

What causes those diseases?

Selfishness, greed, avarice. You know the story of the Nazarene who told the man: "Your sins are forgiven." You must realize that there are both physical and spiritual causes for your disorders. They could all be treated in the same way, but some are more easily treated in the physical way. But, though the etheric body is affected by illness and sometimes even causes illness, there is no real illness in the spiritual body. It is a defect in its adjustment with the body of matter. It would affect its vibrations and its relationship with the body of matter to such an extent that disease would begin in the body of matter. Anger can affect the spleen. Jealousy can affect the liver.

Those things cause maladjustment. The perfect balance is distorted and the harmony is upset. When the body becomes so diseased that the balance is completely upset, then the body of spirit is compelled to sever itself because it can no longer express itself through that body, and death takes place.

If a person lost an arm of the physical body, how would that affect the etheric body?

There is nothing that would happen to the arm of the etheric body, but there would be a lack of adjustment between the two arms. The etheric arm could not function while you were in the body of matter. You have never heard us say that any case is hopeless. There is always hope. But there are many factors that have to be taken into consideration.

There is the body of matter, the body of spirit and the vital cord or lifeline between them. As disease, infirmity, or age creep over the body of matter, there is a gradual loosening in the adjustment between the two bodies, because the severance from the world of matter is gradually being effected. There are three causes of disease—physical, mental, and spiritual. A broken arm could be set spiritually, but it would be easier to deal with it physically.

How do you reconcile hereditary disease with perfect justice?

You get the body you have earned. You start this life on earth with what you earned in your last life. You start in one incarnation with what you deserved when you ended your last. But hereditary disease does not put you at an unfair disadvantage, because you each have the instrument that will enable you to fulfil what is necessary for your evolution.

* * * * *

Questions and Answers:

SOME people can be healed by mediums, and others are not. Are they different kinds of cases, regarded from the point of view of the evolution of their souls?

No. If they are to pass into my world, there is no healer in your world who can prevent their passing.

But some who go to healers would otherwise pass on.

A few days, more or less, what are they in eternity?

Does not that make healing rather unnecessary?

No, because to express service is to express the Great Spirit. Much of your sickness and disease is not due to the evolution of the soul, but because, in ignorance, man lives contrary to the Law. It is true that he lives contrary to the Law because his soul has not yet reached the state of evolution where he understands the Law. When your soul has so expressed itself in evolution that it is at one with the Law, there is no sickness then.

If two people suffer from a disease, from the same cause, and one is healed while the other is not, does not that seem unjust?

Do you think it is by chance that people go to healers? It is not chance. There is no chance, in your world or in mine. I tell you the Law is perfect. One day you will understand its operations and, like myself, you will be smitten with wonder at the Perfect Love which fashioned the Perfect Law

All of us—and I say this of myself, too—grope in the dark, seeing sometimes a flash of light and an insight into the Law. We wonder, but, because when we are in the dark we do not see the Law, we think of chance, we think of accident. I tell you there is no chance.

I know you will say: "But what about free will?" Yes, you have free will, but is not your free will subject to the evolution of your soul? It is free, but its freedom is regulated by your soul's growth. It is free, but it is chained to the laws of the universe, which control all things. Nothing escapes the Law, whether you point to the mightiest organization in the universe or the tiniest speck of minute life. Nothing escapes the Law. The Law is perfect.

How does spiritual healing operating through a medium differ from magnetic healing by a medium?

They are quite different. Magnetic healing is dependent on the radiations of the medium's own psychic powers. Spiritual healing is dependent upon the instrument being attuned to the vibrations of the spirit, so that rays, which are normally beyond the range of the world of matter, can be sent through the medium.

Is it possible for a cure to be effected upon identical twins suffering identically, after the medical profession has given up hope, by help and assistance from the Other Side?

I cannot say. There is a power of the spirit which can be used for the relief and for the cure of disease, but it is dependent on the fitness of instruments, or mediums, through which to function. You have not reached in your world of matter the zenith of the Great Spirit's power for healing His children. As your instruments evolve, so more of that power can be given through them. It is dependent on your world as much as on ours. We are all mediums. Behind this medium I am. Behind me there are those greater than I, and behind them there are those greater than they. That chain stretches on to infinity.

Silver Birch used these words when he dedicated W. T. Parish's new healing sanctuary at East Sheen, London:

I DEDICATE this temple to the service of the Great Spirit and His children. This is a hallowed spot where the two worlds of matter and spirit merge and become one, where the power of the Great Spirit reveals itself.

I dedicate this temple to all those afflicted in mind, soul and body, to those in torment and trouble, to those who are in the darkness, to those who are tired and weary. They will come here and the light of love will embrace them in its healing rays.

I dedicate this temple to the service of raising up those who are cast down, helping the fallen, giving strength to the weak, courage to the timid, laughter to tired, tear-stained faces.

I ask you to think not so much of the beauty of the building, of the bricks and the mortar, but of the spiritual temple which is the reality.

I ask you to realize that, though there is no majestic steeple and none of the things which men think make a place a house of God, because they have called it so, this is a house of God because His power has blessed it, because it is a repository of His spirit.

Within these four walls great service will be rendered. There will come here, time and time again, those who are cast by the wayside in the battle of life, those who have been broken in body and in spirit, those who are racked with pain and sickness and disease.

They will come as a last hope and here the power of the spirit will bring them new vigour. They will become refreshed and strengthened and all that which prevents their spirits from functioning in a bruised and broken temple will be cast on one side.

The blind will be made to see; the deaf will be made to hear; the cripple will cast away his affliction. New hope will dawn, for the power of the spirit, bringing healing in its train, will enable them to face life again.

More important still, their spirits will be touched. The flame of the Great Spirit which, in many cases, will have burned very low, will become re-kindled, and out of that experience there will come a new realization because they have been touched by the power of the spirit.

To perform that task you require no vestments and no training in the colleges of men, but only the desire to serve, and to express the gifts of the spirit, raising yourself up to become an instrument of the mighty forces which always seek to flow through channels so that they can be used in your world of matter.

A SPIRIT'S VIEW OF GOD

Some Spiritualists have been puzzled by Silver Birch's conception of God. The following questions and answers will help to make his meaning clear:

WHO or what is the Great Spirit? Is it love—the spirit or feeling of love in everything?

The Great Spirit is the natural Law of the universe. The Great Spirit is the creative force behind all life, whether registered in the plane of matter or in the plane of spirit. The Great Spirit is perfect love and perfect wisdom. The Great Spirit pervades all the universe, whether it is that tiny portion known to you or that larger part which, as yet, has not been revealed to earthly gaze.

The Great Spirit fills all life. The Great Spirit is within all beings. The Great Spirit is within all laws. The Great Spirit is the Great Spirit. He is Life. He is Love. He is everything. How can we, who are but the servants, describe the Master? How can we, whose conceptions are puny, describe that which is of immeasurable magnitude?

We are told that God knows when a sparrow falls. How is it possible for God to know of all that happens to all the vast population of the world, not to mention the countless millions who have passed on?

That which is called God is the natural Law of the universe. The Great Spirit is within everything. Everything is the Great Spirit. Because the soul knows itself, the Great Spirit knows the soul. Because the sparrow *is* the Great Spirit, the Great Spirit knows the sparrow. Because the Great Spirit is in the trembling leaf, the trembling leaf is the Great Spirit. Throughout the whole of your world and mine, throughout the universe, even in worlds which are not yet known to you, the laws of the Great Spirit reign supreme. Nothing happens outside those laws; therefore, all is known because all comes within the compass of natural law, which is the Great Spirit.

You say the Great Spirit is in everything, the source of all things—hate and love, wisdom and folly. It seems to follow that the man who does wrong is acting within the laws of the Great Spirit as much as the man who does right; those who preach the gospel of war and hate as much as those who preach peace and love. No one, in fact, can transgress the laws of God because everything is part of those laws. Can you answer this difficulty?

There is perfection and there is imperfection, but imperfection contains within itself the seeds of perfection, for perfection comes from imperfection. Perfection does not come from perfection, but from imperfection.

Life is evolution, it is progress, a striving upward, a development, unfolding, extension, reaching out. What you call good or bad are but stages in the road of life, lines of progress. They are not the end. You judge with an imperfect understanding. You say thus far is good, thus far is bad. That is only your idea. When you are not in relation to these events, you judge them differently. But the Great Spirit is within all things.

Then is the Great Spirit responsible for earthquakes?

The Great Spirit is the Law—the Law that controls all things. The Law governs all things. There is nothing in the universe which is outside the Law.

I know that earthquakes and storms and lightning puzzle the brains of those in your world, but they are all part of the universe. The universe is evolving, even as those who dwell in it are evolving. The world of matter is far from perfect yet—and it will not reach perfection. It will evolve higher and higher.

Does that mean that the Great Spirit is evolving?

No, the Great Spirit is the Law and the Law is perfect. But that part of the Great Spirit that is expressed in your world is subject to the evolution of that world as far as its expression is concerned. Remember that your world is evolving, and these things are the signs of its evolution. Your world was born in fire and tempest and is gradually evolving towards perfection.

You cannot say that the Great Spirit is responsible for the beauty of the sunset and the sunrise, for the myriads of glittering stars in the firmament, for all the delightful songs of birds, and then say that the Great Spirit is not responsible for the storm and the lightning, the thunder and the rain. They are all part of the great law of the Great Spirit.

In that sense, you might argue that the Great Spirit is responsible for those who are depraved, for those who are so unenlightened that they render harm to their brothers in your world.

But to each one of you there is given that amount of free will which, as you evolve, you learn to exercise. The higher you evolve in the spiritual scale, the greater can you exercise your free will. You are your own limitation, but, because you are part of the Great Spirit, you can conquer all the difficulties and obstacles in your world.

Spirit is superior to matter. Spirit is the king and matter is the servant. Spirit reigns supreme. It is the essence out of which all life is made, for spirit is life and life is spirit.

Is there a Great Spirit apart from His universe?

No, the universe is but the reflection of the Great Spirit. The Great Spirit is the system.

Can a fly understand the world? Can the fish realize what the life of the bird is? Can a dog reason like a man? Can the stars understand the sky? Can you understand the Great Spirit, Who is greater than all your minds?

But you can try to learn to express your soul, so that, when no words pass your lips and in the silence of your own soul, your spirit reaches out for communion with the Great Spirit. Then you know that He and you are one. It is not possible to express that in language, but it is expressed in the silence of the soul within you and within every soul in the universe.

Does spirit need contact with the world of matter in order to gain conscious individuality?

Yes. In order to gain consciousness it must incarnate through matter and have the experiences of matter. It evolves from matter into spirit. That means that its association with a body of matter enables it to express itself as an individual working through the personality of the physical. Spirit becomes aware of itself after it has incarnated into matter.

If so, is the Great Spirit gaining experience through us?

No. Your evolution cannot affect that which is already perfect.

But we are all parts of the Great Spirit. Does not the evolution of a part affect the whole?

It only affects that part which is manifesting through you, which in itself is perfect, but is not perfect in its expression through each one of you. In itself, spirit is perfect. It is the primary substance of the universe. It is the breath of life. In its expression through you it is imperfect because you are imperfect. As you evolve, more of the perfection can express itself through you. You are not evolving the spirit, but you are evolving the bodies through which the spirit can express itself.

Are the bodies through which the spirit expresses itself made of matter in varying form?

Yes. The Law is perfect. The Law as it is expressed through

you is not perfect because you are imperfect, and so the perfect Law cannot operate through you. But as you become more and more perfect, so more of the Law can operate through you. Imagine you have a mirror and a light. The mirror reflects the light, but if the mirror is very poor it cannot reflect all the light. As you make the mirror more perfect, it can reflect more of the light.

Everything is constantly working itself out in fuller expression. Have I not told you that life is like gold that has to be extracted painfully from the ore, which has to be crushed and purified? Who is to say that the ore is bad but the gold is good?

But surely we all have ideas of what is good and what is evil.

These are but the expressions of the moment. They express the stage which has been reached in evolution. When the soul has evolved higher, it will leave them behind. They are but the imperfections caused by a perfect law seeking to express itself through instruments which have deviated from the path. That is why I embrace them all.

Does that mean that God, in the beginning, was not good?

I know nothing of beginnings. I know nothing of endings. I only know the Great Spirit always has been and always will be. His laws are perfect in their operation. Do you not see that you may have perfect light but, if you strive to reflect it through badly polished mirrors, it does not emerge as perfect? But you cannot say the light is imperfect, that it is evil. It is only that the soul is not yet ready to express the perfection that is within itself. That which your world calls evil is only imperfection, imperfectly expressing the Great Spirit through it.

Is it right to say there is only one Being or Person that is able to create, and that we have not the power to create anything at all?

The Great Spirit is, always was, always will be. All life is the Great Spirit and the Great Spirit is all life. How can you create? But the more you are evolved in your soul, the more you can beautify and improve. The less evolved you are, the lower is your range in the universe.

THE VALUE OF PRAYER

Speculation on the value of prayer is not confined to Spiritualists. In every religion there are those who wonder whether God hears them when they pray to Him. But few understand that prayer is subject to law, that some prayers are efficacious because they conform to law and others are unanswered because a law has been broken. The following answers to questions will give a more rational view of supplication:

IS it important to pray?

That depends on the prayer. The aimless repetition of words merely creates ripples in the atmosphere, but those who pray with their hearts and their souls, seeking in prayer closer unity with the Great White Spirit, seeking to make themselves useful instruments for His manifestations, emerge, because of prayer, stronger and more fitted to be His servants. The act of prayer, the revealing of oneself, the opening of the heart, binds us all together in unity.

Would you say that prayer produces a result that is only subjective and not objective? A prayer may make you a finer character, but would it have any external result?

True prayer should enable you to equip yourself for service. Prayer is the means by which you attune yourself to higher forces. I do not mean by prayer repeating the words that others have written without a realization of what they mean, but praying with the soul and the mind, with an earnest desire to reach out to the highest the soul can attain. Then, filled with the inspiration that comes as a result of the prayer, you emerge stronger.

Is it of any use praying for somebody else?

Yes, true prayer is never wasted, for thought has potency.

Have the prayers of a healer engaged in absent healing any real effect?

Yes. I was answering your question as it referred to individual prayer, but it also has universal application. By prayer you are releasing psychic energy, and this can be used by guides.

Is it possible through prayer to enlist the help of those in the spirit world when otherwise that help might not be available?

If you pray with sincerity, you make yourselves, because of the act of prayer, accessible to higher forces. The mere act of prayer opens up the soul. You must pray with your hearts, souls and minds. Mere requests are not prayers. Prayer, truly understood, is a great spiritual exercise. I can best explain it all by saying that prayer should always be regarded as a means to an end, not the end itself.

There is only one prayer—that prayer is, "Teach me how to serve." There is no greater work, no greater love, no greater religion, no greater philosophy than that you say "I want to serve the Great White Spirit and His children." It matters not which way you serve, whether by bringing the truth of the spiritual part of the Law, or whether you feed those who are hungry or take away all the darkness in men's hearts. It does not matter which way, so long as you serve.

The more you learn how to forget yourself and to serve others, the more you help to develop the spirit—that is, the Great White Spirit—within each one of you. It is all very simple, but they build churches and say many strange things. They use long words that I do not understand, and have ceremonies which they say help religion.

But all I know is that you must go and lift up those who are falling, give sleep to those who are weary, food to those who are hungry, drink to the thirsty, new light to those who are in darkness. Then the laws of the Great White Spirit are working through you.

Why is it that often prayers seem to be unanswered?

In everyone there is always a war going on between that part which is human and that part which is divine. When that part which is divine wins, then you feel at one with the Great Spirit. When the human part triumphs, then you feel disheartened. Often you have to be guided not into the paths for which you think you are fitted, but into those paths where you can be used to give the greatest service.

Every day and every night there comes into this house a band of spirits. Each one of them has given up his right to progress in order to build here conditions so that one day it will be a circle of light, with its illumination radiating into all the dark places of the earth. Beside that mission, the little troubles of earth are nothing.

Whilst there are people who have no place to put their heads, who have no homes, and have to sleep under the skies of the Great Spirit, with His stars as their only light, their bodies exposed to the storm and the rain, and others who do not get sufficient food to sustain them, do you think the troubles of any one of you are important in the sight of the Great Spirit?

I only ask you to remember that you are all helping the Plan of the Great Spirit, that great and wondrous design in which each one of you is helping to weave your own little pattern. One day the whole fabric will be revealed and every race and every colour will have its part. Then it will become a perfect universe.

What takes place in the silence, when nothing seems to happen, is but a part of the embroidery being woven. Day after day, and night after night, the work goes on, everyone helping to weave a mighty fabric which will one day cover all the children of the earth.

Sometimes you ask for things which are not good for your soul, which will only retard your own progress. Those things cannot be given to you. Sometimes you ask for things which your soul has not earned. They cannot be given to you. Sometimes you ask for things which are already in preparation, ready to be poured into your midst when the right time comes. You must understand that the Great Spirit knows already of the unspoken prayers of all your hearts.

Does prayer, as recited daily in churches, avail anything?

It depends on the one who prays. If it is a prayer of the lips, then it is but an empty waste of sound. If it is a prayer from the soul, a prayer of earnestness and aspiration, a prayer that desires to reach out to the Great Spirit, then the very desire gives it wings which carry it into the heights of the realms of spirit.

Would the prayer of a little child, for example, be of any use in curing a drunken parent?

All sincere prayer carries with it a power. How far that power can be transmuted into a material result depends on many conditions. It depends, in the case that you give, upon the soul of the man, whether that power can touch his soul, or whether he is so far removed from spiritual things that no spiritual thing can touch his soul. I cannot say yes or no to that question.

But it would have some effect?

All prayer which is prayer, which is aspiration, which is desire for service, for knowledge, for light, for wisdom, for guidance, all that prayer is part of the soul's evolution. Your mind is part, not of the body of matter, but of the spirit, the Great Spirit, and it has powers which belong to the Great Spirit. But before you can use those powers you have to learn through your soul evolution. Otherwise, they cannot be revealed to you.

Are prayers heard by an individual in spirit, or must we postulate a power which can only respond to vibrations which harmonize with itself?

Prayer is the expression of the soul. Let me make that clear. It is the yearning of the soul which cries out for light, for guidance. That very act, of itself, brings an answer, because it is setting into motion the power of thought.

It is the cause which attracts a reply, which is the effect. There is no need for any spirit to wait for you to pray, because the quality of your prayer immediately attracts all those on the spiritual plane which your prayer can reach, according to the evolution of your soul.

And naturally their power—because they desire to serve your world—adds to the power which you set up. You have set into motion waves of thought which are part of the spirit. This enables the forces of the universe to work in accordance with your evolution. That means that you have made yourself accessible to those forces which you can reach.

According to the evolution of the people who pray, it may be necessary for them to fix their minds on some ideal. If that helps the soul, I would not deny it. But the Great Spirit, the laws of life, the natural laws of the universe, these are the things that matter.

Because the Great Spirit is perfection, the laws of the Great Spirit are perfect. That part of the Great Spirit that is within you is perfection, seeking to express itself. As you allow it to express itself, through prayer, through service, you are allowing the Great Spirit which is within you to express itself. All things, prayer, service, whatever you seek to do that uplifts a soul, even your own soul, these things are helping in your evolution.

If everything is governed by inexorable law, what is the use of praying to the Great Spirit, for is not prayer a request that the Great Spirit should interfere with the law of His own ordaining on behalf of the one who prays?

That is not prayer as I understand it. Prayer is the desire of a soul to reach out to the Great Spirit. Prayer is the desire to express the Great Spirit and that act enables the soul to express itself and to reach out to planes which before it could not reach. There is no injustice. There is no favouritism. It is merely that the soul equips itself so that it can express more of the Great Spirit and thus receive more of the bounty of the Great Spirit. The bounty of the Great Spirit is infinite and your soul is infinite as you learn to express its infinity.

Why do we ask God to forgive us our sins: for if the Law is broken does not the penalty follow?

Forgiveness does not enable you to make the adjustment, for you must pay the price. But when you pray for forgiveness you are beginning to put yourselves into harmony with the laws of the Great Spirit, for you are beginning to look within yourself and to examine yourself, and that is when real progress begins.

INIQUITY OF ORTHODOXY

Many may think the following remarks on theology are too severe on the Churches, but if they knew the gentle, loving spirit who is Silver Birch they would know that this guide never indicts without reason. His appeal is to Reason, and he does not bow to the "authority" of Orthodoxy.

THE bondage of creeds is one of your world's afflictions. It is worse than pestilence and disease, far worse than the physical sufferings of the body through illness, for it is an affliction of the soul. It puts the spirit in blinkers.

And yet your world clings to creed when it has at its disposal the infinite wisdom of the Great Spirit. There are some who are only happy whilst they are in prison. Liberty is only for those who know how to enjoy liberty. Rejoice that you have escaped from the thraldom of creed. Rejoice, and strive to elevate others that they too may escape.

We give you no creed, no ritual, no ceremony, but only the love of the Great Spirit seeking to express itself through His children. We ask you to follow no book, no dogma, no leader, no authority, no scroll of parchment, no learning, to worship no relic, but only to follow the laws of the Great Spirit, which are the greatest things in the universe. They are the only supreme authority.

Many so-called churches are the relics of the dark ages. The Great White Spirit is not shut up in any building. He is everywhere. They think that because they put a few stones together and make a big steeple, and put in windows with coloured glass, that they please the Great White Spirit.

He is more pleased when the sunshine He has provided

lightens the hearts of His children and when the rain He sends down brings to fruition all the crops He has given to His children. But between His bounty and His children there stand, very often, the Church, the statesmen and the men of finance. All these must be swept away, and today they are being swept away.

Do not think only in terms of the power of the spirit in the past. Remember that the power which operated through the Nazarene is operating once again. Just as those who were the leaders of the churches in that time rejected that power of the spirit, and said it was of the Devil, so once again they reject the same power of the spirit as it operates today. But your world has evolved, for they do not crucify any longer.

The splendour of the Nazarene does not belong only to the past, but to the present. Where do you think he is today? Do you think the story of his life ended in Jerusalem? Where do you think his great spirit would be today, with your world of matter full of distress, trouble and bitterness?

Those who deny us and say we preach the gospel of darkness are in line with the same people who, in the days gone by, made the same accusation against the Nazarene. We come with the same power of the Great Spirit, bringing the same manifestations of the spirit, the same message: "Comfort the mourner, heal the sick, bring light to those who are in darkness, health to the afflicted, strength to the weary, knowledge to the ignorant."

We are all the servants of the Great Spirit. Some of us have evolved a little higher. Because of that, we return to give service, for service is the law of life. Where there is no service, there is desolation. Where there is service, there is peace and happiness. Your world must build a new system of life with service to one another. It is all very simple, but they make it so hard.

I feel sorry for those "men of God" who have so much to

unlearn. They have built a structure based on shifting sands and they try to defend their sandy castles against the onslaught of spirit truths. They have built falsely. They have surrounded the Nazarene with fable. They have magnified him into the Great Spirit of life and, because the foundation is a faulty one, they have gradually to destroy it. As they destroy, fear strikes their hearts.

They think there can be nothing left at all, whereas the truth is that, if they had built on the foundation of fact, of natural law, there would be nothing to destroy.

That is why we have come back to your world—to ask you to give no obedience to any one man, to any one book, to any one church, to any leader, to any being whether in the world of matter or in the world of spirit, but only to learn obedience to the laws of the Great Spirit, for they alone are infallible and unerringly right.

That is why we preach the natural laws, and the natural laws only. If you call that Spiritualism it does not matter, as long as what you understand embraces the natural laws of the Great Spirit and their operation throughout all the spheres of life, whether life that is visible to you or life as it is known in the planes of spirit.

Your world has set its store by leaders, and has magnified them out of their true importance, and so it has created difficulties of theology—difficulties with scientists, with philosophers and with all those honest people who want their minds to be free and who cannot accept anything which makes their reason revolt.

That is why we emphasize the laws of the Great Spirit, for the true understanding of these laws harmonizes all knowledge. They cannot in any way cause the minds of scientists, philosophers, free-thinkers or anybody to revolt, for they are founded upon eternal, unalterable, immutable operations of the Great Spirit.

You see the wisdom of the counsel that is given to us to express. As your world grows in wisdom and understanding, its people will learn to regulate their lives according to the laws of the Great Spirit. They will learn to have obedience to the Law. They will learn that all the misery and the starvation, the suffering and the heartbreaks that come through your worldly conditions are all caused because the Law is not obeyed.

When the fuller understanding comes, there will be swept away all the hideous growths in the garden of the Great Spirit that prevent its beauty being shown to every one of His children. With that aim we strive, not only to make the souls of mankind free, not only to liberate their minds, but to give their bodies of matter a chance to live in harmony with the laws of the Great Spirit.

I am impatient with Churches because they do not use their opportunities to reveal the great truths that the world of matter has known.

I am impatient because they betray the Nazarene whom they seek to serve.

I am impatient because they remove him so far from humanity that he ceases to be an example and becomes a god, dwelling in the high heavens beyond the reach of the children of matter.

Over the doors of the churches is not written: "We are loyal to truth and truth alone." Rather does it say: "We preach a creed, we espouse a doctrine, we practise ritual, we are tied to ceremony." The Churches are the means of opposing truth.

I do not criticize the many great souls who strive to serve by becoming clergymen. There are many such. I criticize the system that cannot make way for truth, that is loyal only to the old worn-out shibboleths and has no place for the vital, energizing power of the spirit to express itself.

How can the power of the spirit be realized in Churches? They have their prescribed limits to what is allowed to be preached and said.

We teach of the Great Spirit, with natural laws, and are instruments who have revealed the operation of those laws, and we point to the Nazarene and say that he, an instrument of the Great Spirit, was an example of what all the children of matter could reach if they would unfold the power with which the Great Spirit has endowed them.

Creeds, dogmas, doctrines, rituals, ceremony, stained glass, altars, mitre, cope—what have these to do with religion? Religion is in the spirit, the spirit that belongs to all Creation, which expresses itself in every rhythm and manifestation of life, that is revealed in every aspect of Nature and in the striving of all idealists and reformers who wish to serve. What has that to do with a creed?

Learn to be free. Do not imprison yourself. Do not hedge yourself around and refuse to allow new inspiration to come to you. Truth is a constant search. Its boundaries are ever widening, for as the soul evolves the mind responds.

You become free when you realize there is no limitation to knowledge, truth, wisdom, growth. You become free when you discard at once that which you know in your heart is false, that which reason rejects, because your intelligence cries out in revolt. You become free when you are not afraid to discard error in the face of new light.

There is knowledge for all when you are ready to seek knowledge, but *you* must journey on the great adventure. You must be prepared to start on a search where even sometimes the boundaries are not known, sometimes be prepared for hazards and dangers, sometimes be prepared to walk in uncharted territory, yet always prepared to follow truth wherever she leads and to reject all that is false, no matter how old it may be.

Your world pays too much attention to old fables because they are old. Truth and age do not always march together. I know it is difficult to surrender the dearly held beliefs learned in the days of childhood, but when the soul becomes free it must discard all that reason rejects.

How much poorer is your world because it does not learn how to make itself more accessible to the powers of the spirit! How much longer must we go on, trying to break down its doors of superstition and its thick walls of ignorance?

But it will not be as long as you think. Look around and see. There are signs everywhere of decay. The proud citadel is crumbling. One day, when there are enough of you to shout, the walls will tumble down.

Questions and Answers:

WHY are so many of the lives, deaths and resurrections of figureheads of religion, including the Christian religion, similar to those of the mythological gods whose lives were based on the phenomena of nature, such as the solar system and the seasons?

It is because the children of earth have always borrowed from the myths of ancient times in order to invest their leaders with supernatural powers. They did not understand the operation of natural laws. They wanted the one whom they considered to be the greatest of all to be endowed with attributes beyond the reach of the other children of the Great Spirit. And so they have all borrowed from one another.

But that does not affect the teaching which was given by the messengers of the Great Spirit who, each in his own day, reflected some of the truth, wisdom and love of the Great Spirit.

Is it an accident that these lives do, according to their followers, follow the course of nature, many of the recorded incidents in their lives being suggestive of natural law, such as resurrection following death as the spring follows winter?

If you mean the story in the Bible that, when the Nazarene was crucified, there was great thunder and lightning, that is not true. If you mean that all those who die, as your world calls it, return, that is true. I understand the question to refer to the additions to the historical lives of the messengers of the Great Spirit.

What is the sin against the Holy Ghost?

The sin against the Holy Ghost is to deny the Holy Ghost.

What is the Holy Ghost?

It is the power of the spirit which descends into the world of matter. Your Churches worship it in the abstract, but they reject it when it descends on millions all over the world, for it is that power which we use to commune with you. It is that power of the Great Spirit which enables, even for a short time, the world of spirit and the world of matter to become one in harmony of purpose.

I have been told that baptism in any denomination has, as its object, that when a spirit passes over, a band of spirits belonging to that denomination receive it and care for it until it is adjusted to the new conditions. If this is so, what happens to non-baptised souls?

The power that set the universe in motion, the Spirit that breathed into a body the breath of life and made it a living soul, the Great Spirit Who is responsible for all the worlds, for all the laws of the universe, the Great Spirit Who is expressed in life in all its varying degrees, the Great Spirit Who has been revealed throughout all the ages by all the seers and the instruments, the Great Spirit Who is within all, the Great Spirit Who is behind all, is not troubled whether a man has sprinkled water or not.

What does matter is whether the life has been lived in

accordance with his highest ideals. The laws cannot be cheated because a few drops of water are sprinkled on a baby. The laws cannot be altered, for effect always follows cause.

Has not Christianity produced plenty of good men?

They would have been good just the same, whether they were Christians or not.

But are not some good because they try to follow the teachings of Jesus?

When your world emulates the Nazarene, a new chapter will have begun in history. It has not happened yet. I do not see any signs of it. Do not speak to me of "Christians", whose lives mock the one they profess to serve. Did not the Nazarene say: "Not every one that saith unto me, Lord, Lord, shall enter into the kingdom of heaven; but he that doeth the will of my Father which is in heaven"?

Are there not thousands of Christians who believe the creeds superficially and who yet live very good lives and who are unselfish?

They are not good Christians. They are bad Christians, but good men. Remember this, every creed fetters the soul. Men are not good because of creed, but in spite of creed. In the name of creed they have killed one another and they have burned one another. Anything which binds, which cramps the soul, which prevents it from having full expression, must be swept away.

What of priests who go to leper colonies to help the sufferers there?

They do not go because of creed, but because the soul wishes to serve. Religion is beyond creed. Creed is not religion.

A reply to the wireless plea of the Archbishop of Canterbury, who called for a return to organized religion, was given by Silver Birch:

YOUR world has had a "Recall to Religion". Real religion is service to the Great Spirit by serving His children. To do that, you require no churches, no priests, no clergymen, no sacred books—unless they implant in your heart the desire to serve, and make you love the children of the Great Spirit more than you loved them before. Serve whenever you can. Help to lift your brother's load. That is religion.

I only repeat the simple truth that many of you know, either instinctively or else through reason and logic. I bring the truths which I have learned in the larger realm of the spirit, where all people have to face reality, where cause and effect can be seen in their immediate operation, where only those who serve are counted as higher than those who do not. All the pretence and shams of your world are stripped away and the soul is revealed in all its nakedness, so that its strength and its weakness can be known to all.

I come from a world where values are known, where falsity does not exist and inequality does not reign. There are no poor and no rich in my world, except those who are poor or rich in spirit. There are no mighty and no weak, except those whose souls are mighty or weak. When all the things that your world of matter praises highly have faded away into the dust of the forgotten past, the eternal realities of the spirit will endure for ever.

Look around your world of matter, see the misery and the despair, the sorrow and the anguish. Look around and realize that there is a vast field for service. Ignorance still reigns, misused power still prevails, prejudice has still to be overcome.

See the hunger and the starvation, those who "suffer" because they have too much and those who suffer because they have nothing. See the many physical bodies racked with pain, unable to express as they should the power of the Great Spirit within them. See the condition of poverty and distress, the hovels that should shame all those who regard themselves as Christians.

And remember that your world can be a Kingdom of Heaven, that it is filled potentially with all that can transform it into a garden of peace and plenty, but it is choked by the weeds of selfishness.

We call all of you to service, asking you to forget yourselves and your own desires, to allow that which is divine to triumph over that which is earthly, so that each one of you becomes a messenger for the Great Spirit of life. Each one of you should seek to carry on the work of reform, to bring cheer and happiness to all who need it, to wipe away all tears and to replace them with laughter, to fight all ignorance and superstition, to let knowledge reign in their place, to abolish all the darkness and to allow the light of divine truth to penetrate, to banish all fear, all mourning, all disease, so that love can rule triumphant.

While Silver Birch does not regard Jesus of Nazareth as being divine in the unique sense taught by the Church, he always speaks of him with deep reverence as the greatest teacher ever incarnated into the world. Here are some of the questions he has been asked regarding the status of Jesus:

WAS Jesus Christ "God the Son", as the Church says, or was he an ordinary man with great mediumistic powers?

The Nazarene was a messenger of the Great Spirit who came into your world of matter in order to fulfil a mission of the Great Spirit. He fulfilled his mission on earth, but he has not yet fulfilled the rest of his mission, which is still being directed from the world of spirit. It is wrong to worship the Nazarene, for worship should be given only to the Great Spirit and not to His messengers. The Nazarene came into your world by fulfilling the natural laws which the Great Spirit had ordained, the same natural laws which all must fulfil in order to be born into your world. You cannot live, you cannot be born into your world, you cannot pass from your world into mine, except through the natural laws of the Great Spirit.

Can you substantiate that by references to Bible texts?

My appeal is only to the laws of the Great Spirit. Those who rely on the crutches of words must be left until their souls can be awakened to an understanding that the Great Spirit is still at work, still inspiring, still revealing.

His laws are still in operation and His power can flow through instruments today, if they will allow themselves to be used for the Great Spirit, as instruments were used many, many years ago. The Bible, as you call it, is a great book. But there is a greater Bible. It is the universe, which is sustained by the laws of the Great Spirit. From that, you can learn far more than from any book in your world of matter, however great it may be, however respected it may be, however revered it may be.

Where is Jesus now, and what is he doing?

The spirit that worked through the Nazarene is still at work, seeking to continue the work that it started two thousand years ago, but that spirit has been crucified a thousand times since, and is being crucified almost every day. But, because that spirit is part of the Great Spirit, it will continue to spread its influence wherever there are instruments who can work for the Great Spirit to bring peace and happiness to your world of matter.

When you speak of the Nazarene, do you mean the man Jesus or the spirit forces working through him?

The man. But he has since evolved and there is now a far greater spiritual consciousness expressed through him than there was in the earthly incarnation, for the amount that he expressed then had to be in consonance with the limitation of his day. There has never been on earth anyone through whom the manifestation of the spirit has been greater than through the Nazarene. There has never been any through whom the laws have revealed themselves at so great an intensity as through the Nazarene.

Not in two thousand years?

No, neither before nor since. That was the greatest manifestation of the Great Spirit that your world has yet received. But we do not reverence the man as he incarnated on earth. We pay tribute to the power which operated through him. We recognize that the man is only entitled to respect in so far as he was the instrument for the power of the spirit.

Is the spirit world planning a further revelation by the sending of another teacher like Jesus?

Different methods are being used to suit the different needs. You must remember that your world has become more complex, more interdependent, and more channels of communication have had to be opened. We have to meet with different temperaments and different habits, thoughts, ways and modes of life. Our message has to be adapted to national environments and characteristics, to racial habits. It has to be given in the language and the limitations of a variety of peoples. But behind the focus of the power is the same driving force.

Your Christian world pays its tribute to one who rose from the "dead", who was seen after his "death", who demonstrated that life continues beyond "death". The Nazarene demonstrated that he was the same individual and he gave as proofs, in the materialized body, the earthly marks of the crucifixion. After that, he revealed himself again.

Your Christian world believes all that, though it cannot prove it. But it says it was a miracle! We have returned through the same laws to demonstrate the life beyond death, to show that the Great Spirit is eternal and the operation of His laws immutable, that even as one was resurrected so are all resurrected, because resurrection is a law of the Great Spirit of life.

CREEDS v. TRUTH

When the twenty-five theologians who had been examining Church beliefs for fifteen years, in the hope of arriving at some sort of conformity within the Church of England, published their weighty report, "Doctrine In The Church of England", in January, 1938, Silver Birch was asked to comment on some extracts which were read to him. The extracts are printed in italics:

TRUTH is most easily understood when you become as little children and allow your minds to become freed from all the misconceptions that come from the errors of the past.

Truth comes when, like a little child, you seek with simplicity, with the desire not to establish a new creed or doctrine but only to find that which is true, no matter how great the sacrifice involved.

Those who have promised loyalty to certain teachings are not in the best position to find truth, for sometimes the soul struggles hard between its allegiance to that which it has sworn to believe and that for which its mind strives in order to give it satisfaction.

* * * * *

The Resurrection of Jesus is an act of God wholly unique in human history.

Did it take fifteen years to arrive at that conclusion? How true it is that those who betray the Nazarene are those who call themselves Christians!

Resurrection is part of the law of life. Resurrection comes to every soul when it is resurrected from the body of matter when death arrives. Resurrection belongs to no one man. It belongs to all the children of the Great Spirit, for everyone in turn must pass through the portal of death, leaving behind the body of matter, and begin a new life in the realm of spirit, in the body of spirit, which has been preparing itself all the time.

The Nazarene did nothing contrary to natural law. He came to fulfil the Law, and all his actions and all his teachings were part of the Law. Did he not say: "All these things shall ye do and greater things than these shall ye do"? If you elevate the Nazarene to so remote and inaccessible a place in the high heavens that no child of the Great Spirit can reach him, then you have destroyed the whole value of his mission, for the essence of the Nazarene's life was to demonstrate what could be achieved by all the children of the Great Spirit if they would but allow the fullness of the Great Spirit to reveal itself in their lives.

And when he passed to the world of spirit he returned, as many returned before him and as countless thousands have returned since. There is nothing unique in the universe, for the laws of the Great Spirit are always in operation, and the mere fact that anything has ever happened is proof of the existence of law.

* * * * *

Baptism, even infant baptism, is a means of deliverance from the domination of influences which predispose to sin. In the life of the unbaptised saint there is a defect.

No priest possesses the power of magic, to make of water anything but water. Because a priest takes drops of water and sprinkles it on the brow of a child, he does not in any way do anything which affects the child's life in your world or mine. Those drops of water were drops of water before and they were drops of water afterwards. The priest has no power to change their chemical constituents and to make them do something which is contrary to the Law.

The soul is unaffected by baptism, for none has the power to evolve your soul for you. That you must do for yourself, by the quality of the life that you live in the world of matter. The effects of your actions cannot be removed by any other, but only by the compensation that you make and the retribution that you have to suffer.

Saintliness has nothing whatever to do with baptism. Saintliness consists of allowing the Great Spirit to shine through your life, so that you achieve as much of perfection in daily life as you can reach whilst you are in the world of matter.

* * * * *

God could work miracles if He pleased, but the commission is divided as to whether or not miraculous events occur.

Would they have been sure if they had deliberated for another fifteen years? How piteous a spectacle, the blind leading the blind! These are your teachers and they cannot tell you whether or not these things happen! There are no miracles. There never have been miracles. There never will be miracles.

The Great Spirit is the Great Spirit, and the laws of the Great Spirit are perfect in their operation. They were conceived by Perfection. If the Great Spirit has to suspend the laws that Perfection created, then chaos must result. If the Great Spirit has to interfere in the scheme of creation to provide for events which He has not foreseen, then the Great Spirit ceases to be Perfection. The Great Spirit becomes imperfect. If the Great Spirit has to perform a miracle to bestow favours on some, then the Great Spirit is a partial deity and not the Infinite Spirit of all life. How they belittle the Great Spirit with their puny conceptions!

Because they are ignorant of the higher laws, because they do not know the power of the spirit, because they themselves are not touched by that power which comes from our realms, they cannot understand these happenings wrought through mediums.

Because they seem to think that the events of the days of the Nazarene contradict what is known today of the physical laws, they are compelled to think of miracles. Yet, if they understood the operation of the laws of the spirit, they would see that the Great Spirit is the same yesterday, today and for ever, and that His power is available and accessible to all who enable His gifts to be exercised in their lives.

* * * * *

A miracle, if it occurs, is not a breach of order, but expresses the purpose of God, which also determines the order of nature. It is therefore nothing irrational or capricious.

They do not understand that all the laws of the Great Spirit have always been in existence, will always be in existence. You only discover in your world of matter the operation of laws because through your inventions you are enabled to register some of the more subtle phases of universal life. But you have not created anything. You have only discovered that which always was in existence.

It is impossible for something new to be created, for all that is part of creation already exists. Nothing can happen to contradict the laws of the Great Spirit, for all the laws already exist, whether you know of their existence or whether you do not.

It is not necessary for the Great Spirit to create new laws, for all the laws are in existence. All that is necessary for the universe is here now, always has been, always will be. The

Great Spirit, being perfect, has foreseen all that is needed in every stage of existence.

* * * * *

From the Christian standpoint the Bible is unique, as being the inspired record of a unique revelation.

How dark are their minds! How they are engulfed in the inky blackness of superstition! How thick is the wall that surrounds them! How deeply they have entrenched themselves behind the fortress of superstition!

Ever since your world of matter has been the world of matter, teachers have come to reveal the Great Spirit to His children. They have spoken the language of their day. The revelation was adapted to the demands of their day, to the country in which they lived, to the stage of growth and development of the people. It had to be given in such a manner as it was capable of being understood—not too high, so as to be beyond their reach.

But always the process of evolution has been at work and, as the children of the Great Spirit have evolved and grown, so new teachers arose, new seers, new prophets and new visionaries, each with his visions, his dreams, his prophecies, his message, his inspiration, his truth, his teaching adapted to the needs of his day. There is no finality in revelation, for the Great Spirit is perfect.

The revelation of today is in line with the revelation of yesterday. We do not deny the truths taught by the Nazarene. The Nazarene did not deny the truths taught by Moses. And those who will come after us, in the world of your tomorrow, will not deny the truths taught by us today.

But, because the children of tomorrow will be at a higher stage of evolution, the truth that is to be revealed to them must be more progressive than the truth that is revealed to you today.

* * * * *

For him (the Christian), Christ is the one, and the necessary, mediator. Christ's access to the Father was direct; we have our access to the Father through Him.

No. The Great Spirit is within you. You are in the Great Spirit. "The kingdom of heaven is within," taught the Nazarene. How little they know of their own Christian teachings! You are never separated from the Great Spirit. The Great Spirit is never separated from you.

There is nothing you can ever do, no vile crime that you can commit of so degrading an intensity that can ever cut you off from the Great Spirit. The tie that binds you to the Great Spirit is imperishable and therefore you can never be lost.

You approach the Great Spirit direct, as you learn to allow the Great Spirit to express Himself in your lives. Each one of you has a portion of the Great Spirit and you require nobody to stand between you and the Great Spirit of life.

That was not the purpose of the Nazarene. He came to teach the people how to live their lives, that the fullness of the Great Spirit might be expressed.

Theology is the curse of the world of matter. It puts mankind in shackles. It puts his soul in prison. To be freed, he must learn to sever himself from all limiting creeds and restrictive dogmas and to find the unfettered truth that comes in spiritual inspiration. The mind of man cannot exceed the inspiration of the Great Spirit.

* * * * *

The Resurrection confirms man's hope of immortality.

So much to learn! So much to learn! You live because you have part of the Great Spirit within you. Matter only exists because of spirit. Spirit is the eternal reality. Spirit is indestructible, imperishable, immortal, infinite.

You will live beyond the grave, beyond the fire of cremation, because you are spirit. Nothing in the world of matter, nothing in the realms of spirit, can destroy the imperishable divinity which is yours, the gift of life conferred on you by your entry into this world.

Because you are a spirit, you live. Because you are a spirit you survive the grave. Because you are a spirit you will continue to live for ever and for ever. It has nothing to do with any teacher. It is part of your birthright, part of your heritage.

They would seek to limit the Great Spirit, the Divine Architect, the Power which maintains the whole universe in all its multitudinous expressions—to what? To one being who lived for thirty-three years in the world of matter. And they would seek to restrict His bounty to those who espouse a creed. Oh, no! Oh, no! They shame the meaning of the word "Religion". Did they but know it, they make the Nazarene weep tears of bitterness and sorrow, and they continue to crucify him.

You are not the salt of the earth because you call yourselves Christians. You are not the salt of the earth because you belong to a Church. You will not be judged in my world by the label you have worn on earth. Your championship of a creed will not matter. All that will be of any account is one thing—how much of the Great Spirit have you expressed whilst you were on earth?

* * * * *

Fundamental to the Christian doctrine of the Atonement is the conviction that it is essentially the work of God, who, in Christ, reconciles mankind to Himself.

Is this a repetition of the old teaching of the atonement? Does it mean that a jealous and angry god had to be appeased by the blood sacrifice of the one he loved? Does it mean that the Great Spirit is more cruel and more heartless than an angry human being? Does it mean that the Great Spirit demands blood to be shed to reconcile Himself with His children? How pitiable a conception is this of the Great Spirit and of the mission of the Nazarene!

Must blood be shed to appease the Great Spirit, of Whom it was taught by the Nazarene He was full of the love and mercy and gentleness of a loving Father? You are all placed in the world of matter to build your own characters and accomplish your own soul evolution.

If you choose the paths of selfishness you must pay the price. If you choose the paths of service, you receive the reward that comes in the growth of character. It is all fixed by the operation of Law, and not even the greatest of the great teachers can alter the operation of those laws.

All else is a doctrine of cowardice and injustice. If you have done wrong, be a man and pay the price! Do not attempt to shelve your responsibilities on to the back of another. In our world, the saint, the altruist, has reached a higher level than the selfish man because his soul has grown much more. How else could it be? Could one man be selfish and reach, after what you call death, the same level as he who devoted his whole life to service? Is it thus that you would mock the Great Spirit and His perfect justice?

Of course not. Life is what you make it. No matter what your sphere, no matter what your occupation, whether you be born of high or low parentage, whatever your rank or title, your colour or race or nationality, you all have opportunities for service. If you neglect them you pay the price, and none can interfere.

Let me finish by quoting the words of the Nazarene: "That which a man sows he must reap."

Then Silver Birch commented:

I WOULD ask you to compare the simple truths taught by the Nazarene and enunciated by us with the language presented by those who are supposed to be your leaders of religion.

We come to you with a simple message, one that does not do any injustice to your reason, that in no measure is an insult to your intelligence. It brings in its train proof that it is what it claims to be, simple spirit truth.

First we bring you what your world demands—evidence that the ones you love are still by your side and that "death" makes no division.

Then we reveal that the power of the spirit inspires instruments who uplift humanity. It comes with a richness in all its fields of labour, seeking to make life sweeter and more harmonious.

Then we bring the rays of healing to alleviate the distress of bodies racked in pain and anguish. We strive to do everything within our power to demonstrate that ours is a divine mission, intended to point the way for all of you to live lives of service.

We repeat the truths taught in other days by those who received a measure of inspiration. We point to the laws of the Great Spirit and show how they have always been in operation. And, using those same laws, we repeat today the phenomena that occurred yesterday.

And yet those who should make themselves accessible to all this power of the spirit refuse to allow it to reach them. They hide themselves in the secluded convents of theology. They enclose themselves in the monasteries of creedalism.

They are afraid, for they know that once all this truth is available to every child of the Great Spirit you have no need for priest or clergyman or bishop or archbishop. You can learn how to enable yourselves to become the instruments of the Great Spirit.

The few things you have told me are added confirmation that the power of creedalism is waning and that our mission is succeeding.

CHILDREN OF EVOLUTION

While theologians preach that man "fell" from a state of grace, Silver Birch expresses the spirit teaching that man has risen and has evolved. He declares that in evolution finality is never reached.

JUST as the seed is put into darkness, there to gain strength before it can burst into life, the seed of human life is put into darkness to obtain the strength of human experience before it can burst into the life of the spirit.

All the experiences of human life are part of the great scheme. Those experiences which you like least of all—sadness, bitterness, tears, disappointments, suffering and pain—are very valuable for your souls.

But you cannot realize that at the time. It is only when you can look back on the whole, and not judge by the part, that you can get a clear picture of the values of life. Through all your adversities the character is tried. Through tears and sorrow the soul is strengthened.

We look at life not through physical eyes but with the knowledge of spirit life, where the true balance is struck. Those who live wisely are the ones who seek to turn all experiences into advantage to their souls, who do not try to flee from trial and temptation but seek to use the innermost strength to face difficulties, for it is in that spirit that character is evolved and strengthened.

The Law is perfect, automatic in its operation. Nobody can evade the Law. Even free will is a law, and its operation is known to those who can see because they have reached that stage of evolution.

You can only exercise your free will according to the stage of evolution you have reached. It would be impossible for you to do anything but that which you do, because it is determined by the stage of evolution of your soul.

You are part of the Great Spirit and have an infinity of divinity to express. As that divinity is expressed, so you become accessible to higher laws—which do not contravene other laws, but are only accessible to you as your evolution unfolds.

There is no limit in infinity. There is no limit to the perfection of beauty, to the splendour of music, and the higher the soul is raised in the scale of evolution, the greater is the world of beauty and harmony available to it. As you rise, so a greater field of harmony awaits the evolved soul.

You are not conscious of the higher whilst you are in the lower, but you are conscious of the lower whilst you are in the higher. Whilst all the laws that control every aspect of that harmony are automatic in their operation, they are not available to you until you have reached them by soul growth.

Your past growth places you in the position of choosing future growth. But you can delay it. What you will do at any moment is determined by the interplay of laws, each of which is automatic in its operation. And your choice is determined by the way that your consciousness responds at that stage of evolution. The soul, if it is aware of itself, chooses that which will advance its evolution.

You can only delay the physical consciousness expressed through your physical brain.

You learn natural law through the evolution of your own spirit. You learn first of all to discard all that which is false, all that which makes your reason revolt, all that which is not in consonance with the love and the wisdom of the Great Spirit.

Before you learn, you must unlearn. You must discard all

that which hinders your minds from thinking as they should. Thus your soul and your spirit grow and you are ready for higher knowledge.

When you meet at séances, your soul is developing and you are becoming more accessible to the infinite wisdom of the Great Spirit. You are learning about the operation of laws that control spiritual phenomena.

You are being taught about the operation of natural laws in relationship to the life that you live. As you fit yourself by progress so greater knowledge comes to you.

I, whom you call Silver Birch, represent only a small portion of the knowledge that belongs to the infinity of the spheres. As you grow, other teachers greater than I can use me to impart higher knowledge and wisdom to you.

There is no final stage. There is no perfection. You are evolving and I am, and those higher than I say that there are working behind them higher ones still.

There is no final height, for if you achieved the end, creation would cease.

For many millions of years you have evolved your body or matter, changing slowly but gradually from lower to higher states, evolving, reaching out, climbing out of the mud towards the skies.

Slowly, the beast has been left behind and the Great Spirit has begun to emerge. How many millions of years has it taken you to reach what you are today in your bodies of matter? And that evolution is not yet finished. How many millions of years can you spend in the evolution of your souls?

Not long ago, you were monkeys—not the monkeys, actually, but the spirit which works through them. It is all part of the Great Spirit. Wherever you have life, you have the breath of the Great Spirit, otherwise there would not be life. There are grades of that breath. There is development and unfoldment, there is transition from the lower to the higher.

But it is all the breath of the Great Spirit. That is why the lowest form of life in the lowest part of the world of matter is linked with the Great Spirit and with the highest saint who ever trod the earth, because of the breath of the Great Spirit within them all. The worst criminal in your world and the most beautiful soul are brothers, because of that breath of the Great Spirit within them all. You cannot escape the Law. That is why you are all responsible for each other.

There is a "group spirit" of each species. It is not you who have been the monkey, the fish or the bird, but the spirit which works through you, of which you are a part.

* * * * *

The guide has been asked many questions on evolution A selection from them, with his answers, are printed here:

WHY are children born with defects, such as being crippled or blind, through no fault of their own?

You must not judge the soul from without. You must not confuse the evolution of the soul with the evolution of the body which it uses on your plane.

Although there is what you call a defect, which is caused by the natural law of inheritance from the father or the mother, or both, it does not interfere with the soul's evolution.

You will find, usually, that those who start their material lives with a material defect have in their souls a compensating principle. They exhibit in their characters more kindness, toleration and gentleness to others. There is an eternal principle of compensation. There is nothing that escapes the law of cause and effect.

Because those who are the physical parents have the responsibility of providing the materials for the bodies of the coming race, it is their duty to hand on that which should be as perfect as possible. But, if they neglect their responsibilities, the Law cannot be altered.

If a person is insane and is not a responsible being, how does he get on when he passes to the Other Side, since we are all judged by our characters and the manner in which we have stood our tests?

You confuse the things of matter with the things of spirit. When the brain cells are out of order, they cause confusion in your world. The soul knows its own responsibility even if it cannot express itself in your world because the machinery has gone wrong.

The laws of the Great Spirit work according to the evolution of the soul. The soul is not judged from the standards of earth, but from the standards of eternal wisdom. The soul that wrongs your worldly standard may be judged wrongly from your worldly standards, but if a soul is not responsible, then it is not accounted in the spirit life as in your world.

It is the same with those, who, in moments of madness, as you call it, take others' lives or their own. They cannot be blamed because the machinery has gone wrong. In my world, the true standard is the standard of the soul's motive. Where that is concerned, there is no mistake.

If the soul has been unable to learn its lessons in its life on earth, because of the defective machinery, what is its position in the spirit world?

To that extent, it has lost the earthly experience because through the machinery being wrong it does not register its experiences on the soul as it should. It has lost the value of physical experience. But the principle of compensation is at work all the time.

We take into the next world the character we form through

passing through the various tests on earth. In the case of an insane person, is he judged by the character he has formed?

He is judged only by his own soul evolution and the motives of his soul.

In our world, some children are born in a slum atmosphere of drink, mental, moral and physical filth, and are faced with a life of hard, monotonous labour, while others grow up surrounded by beautiful things and have a delightful preparation for life. How is the unfairness of such cases taken into account?

The soul registers its own evolution. People in your world judge always by material standards and not by the expression of the soul. To all, whether born in low or high estate, come opportunities for service, for the soul to find itself and to express its own divinity. That is the only standard of judgment. All things in your world, judged by a material standard, seem to produce inequalities, but the true compensation is the compensation of the soul, which learns to express itself through all difficulties.

But why does a bad person have a good time?

You judge once again by your worldly standards. How do you know that the soul of the one who has a good time is not miserable, is not tortured, is not racked with anguish and pain? Because you see a smiling face, because you see luxury surround that person? Do purple and fine linen go hand in hand with a satisfied soul? Eternal standards are the standards of the spirit, if not of the world of matter. Otherwise there would be no justice.

But surely it is easier for a soul to express good motives when surrounded by a good environment, rather than in surroundings where sin, hunger and everything that is low predominate?

I do not agree with you, because I see that nearly always the great souls of your world have been born of low estate. All the great masters of your world have come from low estate. The more difficulties that the soul has to struggle against, the greater the soul can become. It is in the struggle against circumstances that the soul comes into its own. Try to judge not from without but from within.

Has the human spirit evolved simultaneously with the evolution of physical life?

It has evolved, but not on the same pathway, because it was necessary for a certain amount of evolution to take place in the physical body before the spirit could express itself.

As we can progress after "death" if we will, is it possible to sink to a lower level by sinful motives after "death"?

Oh, yes. There are many who do not progress for hundreds and sometimes thousands of years who are still filled with the desires of earth even when they have passed to the world of spirit. Their lives are filled with greed and desire, and they seek not to understand the laws of the spirit.

The things of the spirit make no impression upon them, for they are still of the earth earthy and they sink from lower planes to still lower planes.

Does a soul ever sink so low that it is extinguished altogether?

No. It may reach a stage where the spark of the Great Spirit within it is but a small flicker, but the light never goes out, for the link which binds it to the Great Spirit is a link forged in eternity. No soul descends so low that it cannot rise. No soul is so high that it cannot descend to help the lowest.

Does the individual lose his or her individuality after passing through the various spheres, eventually merging with the Great Spirit, and then being redistributed in various forms through material and other substances?

I know of none that has yet reached a stage so perfect that he can be merged into Perfection. The more you perfect yourself, the more you find still to be perfected, for you are allowing more of your consciousness to be revealed. Because your consciousness is part of the Great Spirit it is infinite, always stretching out to reach to infinity. We know nothing of ultimate perfection.

Is it not a fact that, as individuals progress, they tend to become merged into group personalities, losing their own identity in that of the group?

Not as far as I know. What does happen is that, in order for certain work to be accomplished, those who are of one mind pool their knowledge and their resources, allowing one to act as their spokesman on behalf of the rest. While that happens, they all sink their identity into the one, but that is only temporary.

Have you any knowledge of the survival of lower animals, other than pets?

Yes, I have. There were many animals which were friends of ours when we lived on earth and who were, to us, what your dogs and your cats are to you. These animals, where they learned to express a personality, survived with us. But that survival is not eternal. It lasts only for a time, and then the animal goes on to merge with the group spirit which perpetuates the species. You must understand that all the children of the Great Spirit, because they have the power of the Great Spirit, can transmit the power to survive the change called death to those whose consciousness has not yet been expressed in evolution. You can make it possible for the evolution to express itself before its time because of the love that you show.

Apart from pets, do animals survive individually?

No.

If animals, not pets, do not survive individually, what relationship exists between the Great Spirit and, say, an uncared-for and perhaps ill-treated animal? How does the life of such an animal reveal the love or the justice of the Great Spirit, viewing it as a matter between the Creator and the created?

It is very hard to explain to people in your world things

which are so far beyond their understanding. I have tried to explain that animals, when they pass on, go to join the group spirit, but even then there is a principle of compensation. They are able to work out in divine justice all that compensation which is due to them, but it is on different lines from that of the human evolution.

You may as well try to explain what is the difference between a flower that is cared for and a flower that fades and is allowed to fade because it is given no attention. You cannot understand the law behind that, but there is one just the same.

Are animals compensated individually?

No, in the group. The suffering brings forward the evolution of the group.

If there are in one group animals which have been ill-treated and animals that have not, and the group is treated as a group, it is difficult to understand how part of the group can get more compensation than another part.

Each group is made up of those who have gone through similar experiences.

Do you mean there are separate groups for those who have been badly treated and those who have not?

There are divisions that make up a whole, as you have a body with many forms of cell life as part of that body.

What reason is conceivable for the existence of the lowest forms of life, and how is their creation and necessary destruction compatible with a universe ruled by Love?

Man has free will. He can make the world of matter a Garden of Eden, if he chooses, by exercising the power which the Great Spirit has given him and by using the wisdom which the Great Spirit has given him to discern between the things that are right and the things that are wrong.

If, instead of making it a Garden of Eden, he chooses to allow dirt and filth to exist, why should the Great Spirit be blamed for the results of man's filthiness?

Where is the evidence of God's goodness and love when creation has come through a blood-red track of carnage in its evolution?

Why do they look only at one little corner of the picture and not at the whole picture? Because there is evolution, is that not proof of the God of love? Has that never occurred to them? Because you evolve from the lower to the higher, is that not proof that the force which is behind the Law is a force of love?

Why does God allow earthquakes and volcanoes?

When you say: "Why does God allow?" you must remember that you are trying to question the operation of natural law. I only seek to teach the Law and the experiences I have had of the Law. What you call earthquakes are part of the cleansing process in the evolution of the material world. The world of matter has not yet reached a stage of perfection in evolution.

In that case, thousands of innocent victims have to suffer because of the earth's evolution. Is that just?

I do not see that what you call death is a disaster. To me, it is the great hour of freedom for the soul.

Do you mean that all the people killed in earthquakes are at that particular stage where they are ready for death?

Yes, but they are there because of what has happened in their past lives in your world.

Are there other worlds inhabited by human beings more—or less—advanced spiritually than ourselves?

Oh, yes. There are plenty of worlds inhabited by those who are in advance of your world of matter. This planet you call earth is only one of many planets in the vast universe. There is one planet less spiritually advanced than you.

Why is it that sometimes we want to follow a line of our work that we think is important and we find continual obstruction to our plans?

All the things that are worth doing and worth achieving are

those that are the most difficult to perform. The path of attainment is not an easy one. It is full of difficulties, of obstructions, of hamperings that come in the way.

Those things are part of the building of character, so that in the way you face your difficulties is determined the growth of the soul. If you could allow the highest that is within you to express itself without difficulty, it would have little value.

Do not despair. Remember there is no difficulty or obstacle that crosses your path that is so strong that you cannot overcome it by the use of the latent powers that you have within you. Even the difficulties that others place in your path can be swept aside if you will but allow all that is within you to rise and become the master.

Your world does not understand that you express so little of yourself while you are in the world of matter.

Of what use is the earth life of all the countless millions of human babies who perish at, or soon after, birth by infanticide or otherwise?

As long as people judge eternal principles by material standards they will never understand these things. The wisest of your wise do not see beyond earthly knowledge. When the light of spiritual knowledge reaches them through their evolution, then they will see the Plan which is, as yet, not revealed to them. They see through a glass darkly, and so they do not understand.

Would you attempt to judge the life of a schoolboy only by the years that he goes to school, and ignore that greater life which starts beyond his school? There is a greater life than the one in which you live—a world of beauty, a world of colour, a world of love, a world of labour, a world where every sincere desire finds expression, where every creative impulse can express itself, where everything that cannot be fulfilled in your world is able to realize itself. Until you have seen this world, you cannot criticize the Great Spirit.

Those high spirits with whom you take counsel, do they sometimes come here?

No. They are all links in a great chain. As my medium is a link between you and me, and I am a link between you and those beyond me, so they are links between me and those who are beyond them. So it stretches into the inner realms of spirit, much further than my eyes can reach.

Will we ever reach the very highest of all?

No. You do not understand. In your world, you can only manifest a small portion of yourself. You cannot express the whole of your soul because it does not yet possess a vehicle of expression. The more I go back into the inner spheres, the more I express of that which is me. That is why we go back at Christmas and at Easter, to get something of our real individuality.

You are all children of evolution. That is why you mourn. You should remember that those you love go to express more of themselves in my world.

But why do they go so soon sometimes? It seems they could not have learned their lessons.

They leave your world because a law has been broken. It is only through the bitter crucible of experience that the children of earth will learn, in time, the lessons of the Great Spirit.

If it were all easy, then men would not want to work out their own salvation. Then, in a few generations, you would have nothing in your world through which the Great Spirit could manifest. The soul that goes through the agony of pain, illness, bitterness and sorrow, comes out a greater soul, a soul that understands the sufferings of others.

The soul that lives only in its own butterfly happiness and chases always the illusion and the shadow, one day must learn to touch reality. Do not envy those who you think have an easy time. The hardest road in their life is yet before them.

The children of earth must go through every experience, either in your world or mine. There is a lesson to be learned in everything. You do not reach out and create a vehicle in which to enter that inner perfection until you have emerged triumphant from every experience.

It is hard. Why should it not be hard? Should it be easy to become a saint or a martyr, to be a leader or to be a reformer? Why should it be? The soul that seeks to escape responsibility is not worthy of leading.

LIFE IN THE BEYOND

Silver Birch has described something of the beauties of the spirit world, which he declares we visit frequently in our sleep, although most of us cannot remember our experiences on waking:

WHEN you have tasted and enjoyed with your full consciousness all that my world has to offer, you will realize that it is the love we bear for you that makes us come back to work amongst you.

You have not tasted the joys of the world of spirit. There is nothing in your world of matter with which you can compare the life of the spirit, freed from the trammels of the flesh, escaped from the prison of the body of matter, with liberty to go where you will, to see your thoughts take shape, to follow out the desires of your heart, to be freed from the troubles of money. No, you have not tasted the joys of the world of spirit.

You who are encased in matter, do not yet comprehend beauty as it can be. You have not seen our light, colour, scenery, trees, birds, rivers, streams, mountains, flowers—and yet your world fears death.

Death strikes terror into their hearts. But you will only begin to live when you are "dead". Now you live, but in reality you are almost dead. So many are dead to the things of the spirit. The little life-force flickers in their puny bodies, but no spiritual things can find any response within them. But gradually we make progress. Gradually the force of the spirit increases in strength all over your world of matter.

Gradually darkness retreats, as it must when confronted by the light of spiritual truth.

There are no words to compare the life in your world of matter with the life in the world of spirit. We who are "dead" know so much more of life than you do.

This is the world where the artist finds all his dreams come true, where the painter and the poet realize their ambition, where genius has full power of expression, where the repressions of earth are swept away and all gifts and talents are used in the service of one another.

This is the world where there are no clumsy words to express inspiration, but where thought is the living language and reveals itself with lightning rapidity.

This is the world where we have no money to worry us where there is no competition, no driving of the weaker to, the wall, where the strong are strong because they have something to give to those less fortunate than themselves.

We have no unemployment, we have no slums, we have no selfishness. We have no sects, we have only one religion. We have no sacred books, only the operation of the divine laws to instruct us.

And the nearer you get to the belt of matter, the more clumsy and difficult it is for the spirit to express itself. I never like to come back. The only things that make me do so are the promise that I have given to serve and the love of all of you, which gives me some compensation.

To die is not tragic. To live in your world is tragic. To see the garden of the Great Spirit choked with the weeds of selfishness and greed and avarice, that is tragedy.

To die is to enjoy freedom of the spirit, which has been imprisoned behind the bars of the material body. Is it tragic to be released from suffering, for the soul to come into its own? Is it tragic to see wonders of colour, to hear music that does not belong to material expression? Do you call it tragic to express yourself in a body that has no pain, to be able to roam all over the world of matter in a flash and to taste the beauties of the spirit life too?

There is not in your world one artist who could capture with his paints some of the glories of my world. There is not one musician who could record some of the glories of the music sphere with your notes. There is not one writer who could describe in physical words the beauty of parts of this world.

What a pleasant surprise you will all have one day, when you become conscious of our world.

Your world is in beauty now. [**This sitting was held in May.**] You see all around you the manifestations of the Great Spirit, as the dawn of life sweeps over your surroundings again in its cycle, and you marvel at the beauty of the blossom and the fragrance of the flowers, and you say: "How great is the handiwork of the Great Spirit."

And yet, that which you see is but a very, very pale reflection of the beauties that we have in our world of spirit. We have flowers such as you have never seen, we have colours such as your eye has never beheld, we have scenes and forests, we have birds and plants, we have streams and mountains. You have nothing to compare them with. And you will be able to enjoy them, for, even though you will be ghosts, you will be real ones.

You come to our world now, but you do not remember. You visit the spirit world every night. That is your preparation. Otherwise, it would be such a shock when you come here to start your real life in earnest. When you pass on, you will remember your visits.

You will then be freed from the limitation of the body and you will be able to express to the full all the consciousness which has been released during your sleep. In its new expression, it will bring to you all the memories that you have, the memories of all the experiences that you have enjoyed.

* * * * *

Questions and Answers:

WHAT will be the position of those who, after passing, go to the lower planes of spirit life? Will they remember their sleep visits—presumably to the lower planes—and will that memory help them to adjust their position?

Those who would gravitate to the lower planes go to those planes during sleep, but the memory of that would not help them to realize their position after death because the planes on which they found themselves would still resemble the material world.

The lower in the world of spirit, the more earthly it is in appearance because the vibrations are more gross; the higher in the realm of spirit, the finer the vibrations.

Do we sometimes remember our sleep adventures in this life?

When your spirit is released from its body, you are freed from your brain, which is your limitation in the world of matter. The consciousness now has experiences on our vibrations, according to your grade of evolution, and it is conscious of its experiences while it has them. But, when you go back to your body of matter and try to capture the experiences of the spirit, you cannot do so because one is greater than the other. The smaller cannot hold the greater and you get distortion.

It is as if you had a little bag and you tried to get lots of things into it. You could only get some of the things into the bag, and the more you pushed the more out of shape they would become. That is what happens to you when you return to your bodies. But, if your soul is already evolved and you have reached an advanced stage of consciousness, then you are aware of the spirit realms. Then you can quite easily train the brain to remember.

I talk with all of you and I often say: "Remember this when you go back to your world." But you do not. I have been with each one of you and I have taken you to many places. But, though you do not remember it now, none of it is ever wasted.

Do you mean that the memory of these experiences will help us when we pass on?

Yes. Nothing is wasted. The Law is perfect. Those of us who have lived for many years marvel at the perfection of the Law, and when we hear the puny minds of your world criticize the Great Spirit—how little they know! The less they know, the more they express themselves.

Are many people engaged in working during their sleep-state, or are the visits used solely for preparation for the larger life?

Some of you do work, because there are many that you can help in your sleep-state. But, usually, it is a preparation. You are taken to those places which will help you to be ready for your work when you leave the world of matter. If that were not done, the shock of coming from one sphere of expression to another would be so great that it would take you a long time to recover.

That is why it is easier for those who have knowledge when they come to our world. Others have to sleep and rest for a long time, until they can adjust themselves. If you have knowledge, then you pass from one state to another and you are aware of the new life. After all, it is just like opening a door and coming into the sunshine. You must get accustomed to the light.

Those without knowledge would have to have a long period of rest to recover from the period of transition. It is the same as a baby in your world. It has to feel its way. They would still remember their experiences, but more as you remember dreams.

Nothing is ever lost, in your world or in mine. Always remember that. Every thought, every action, every desire to serve that is thrown out of your hearts helps someone somewhere. Always, when the desire is there, you attract those who can help you.

When people pass on lacking understanding, do they respond to our thoughts and receive our mental messages?

Awakening only comes when realization dawns. If you have knowledge, then your awakening is much quicker. We have to fight ignorance, misunderstanding, superstition, false creeds, erroneous theologies, all of which do not help to prepare the soul for its new life. Before these are conquered, the soul has gradually to accustom itself and there is a long period of rest.

As in your world you have hospitals for bruised and injured bodies, we have to treat bruised and injured souls. But where an individual has rendered great service, and love, good will, affection and prayer accompany his passing into my world, then the awakening is speeded, for all those vibrations help him.

What will happen to a person who passes on, not believing in Survival, but thinking that when he dies it is the end?

As you cannot die, because it is contrary to the natural law, that person will have to wake up and face the fact. How long it will take for the realization of spirit life to come to him will depend upon the evolution of his soul—how far it is advanced and how it can attune itself to the new conditions.

Will the passing of such a person be difficult?

That, again, depends on the evolution of the soul. The passing from your world to mine is not difficult, as a rule, because usually the one who passes is not conscious of the change at the time. It is only advanced souls who register the passing out of the world of matter into the world of spirit.

If such a person has been good, will he suffer in any way for not believing the truth of Survival, even if he has been told of it?

Good, bad, I do not know what these words mean. It will depend only upon the life he has led, the service he has rendered, the opportunities he has taken to unfold the Great Spirit that is within him. That is all that counts. It is better to have knowledge than ignorance, but the only test is the way you have lived your life from day to day.

In the spirit life, do we join again with those we love and become younger? Jesus says there is no marriage or giving in marriage.

Wherever there has been love between a man and a woman and that love has brought them together and made them as one, and they have lived on the same spiritual plane in your world, then "death" will not part them. "Death" will be a door which will give them a greater freedom for their souls to be more closely united than they were in your world of matter.

But if their coming together, their marriage as you call it, was not a marriage of souls but only of bodies, and their souls did not dwell on the same plane, then "death" will drive them further apart, for it will relegate them to their own spiritual spheres. If there is love, they will find that in the world of spirit they will get not younger, not older, but will experience growth, evolution, development. These are things of the soul, not the body.

When the Nazarene said that there is no marriage and no giving in marriage, he was referring to the marriage of bodies, not the marriage of souls. For that which you call male and that which you call female each has its contribution to make to each other. The female is necessary to the male and the male is necessary to the female. The Great Spirit embodies the two principles in perfection. As you evolve in the planes of spirit the difference becomes less and less.

Is it possible to sin on the Other Side. If so, what is the most common form of sin?

Of course it is possible to sin in our world. The sins of the spirit world are the sins of selfishness, but in our world they are speedily revealed. They are known as soon as the thought is in the mind, and the effect is seen far more quickly than it is in your world of matter. It registers on the one who commits the sin and makes him spiritually lower than he was before. It is difficult to define more clearly in your language what these sins are, except that they are sins of selfishness.

The heavens or spirit spheres are, relatively to this earth, real and substantial, ruled over by wise chiefs, lords or gods. Has a history of these heavenly kingdoms been made known to us earth dwellers?

There have been many to whom the organization of the world of spirit has been revealed, but we do not have spheres with chiefs. The only chiefs are natural laws. The world of spirit is not a world where spheres are marked off with boundaries such as you have. It is a progressive life from lower to higher stages, with no boundaries, because they all merge into one another. As the soul gradually unfolds, it expresses itself on higher planes of spirit.

If a person is compelled to live a life of loneliness on this earth, is he compelled to lead that life after death?

Oh, no. The Law is always perfect. The soul reaps its own reward and makes its own punishment. Those who are attracted by love and by affection will meet because their souls will throw them together on that plane.

Will it be possible to meet, in the spirit world, great geniuses for whom we might feel a strong attraction, such as Beethoven, Shakespeare and Michael Angelo?

In most cases it will, because wherever there is love by the people of your world for one who helped your world, that creates a natural bond of sympathy which will draw them together in the world of spirit.

When we pass out of the physical body, is the one we use in the spirit world as real and solid as the one we leave behind?

Far more real and far more solid than the one that you leave behind in the world of matter, for your world is not the real world at all. It is only the shadow cast by the world of spirit. Ours is the reality and you will not understand reality until you pass into the world of spirit.

Is the spirit world as natural and as material to the spiritual senses as the physical is to our present senses?

Far more, for this is reality. You are at present prisoners. You are hampered by the material body to which you are restricted on all sides. You are only expressing a very small portion of your real selves.

Do you converse mentally in the spirit world, or is language as we understand it used?

Until people learn how to commune without speech. speech is used.

If one passes suddenly, will he be able to attune himself easily to his new environment?

That depends on the evolution of the soul.

What exactly happens at death, just after the breath has left the body?

When the soul is conscious, it sees the spirit body withdrawing gradually and it opens its eyes in the world of spirit. It is conscious of those who have come to welcome it and it is ready to start its new life. When the soul is not conscious, it is helped through the passage and is taken to whatever place is necessary—it may be a hospital or a home of rest—until it is ready for it to become aware of its new life.

Shall we be with those we love in the spirit world, although separated by convention in the physical world?

It is impossible to separate love from its beloved.

When we enter the spirit world after leaving this life, do we meet our relatives who have passed on before?

If love exists between them, yes. If loves does not exist between them, no.

Is the life on the Other Side everlasting?

All life is everlasting, for life belongs to the Great Spirit, Who is eternal.

Do the spheres of the etheric country in which you live surround the earth or sun or planets?

They do not surround any of them. They are not bounded by geographical distinctions. They are not located in forms of spheres or planets. They are part of the vast universe. They blend and interblend with all phases of life experienced in all planes of life. Some of these planes you know about. Others you do not know yet, for there are planets on which there is life as yet unknown to your world.

Does the fabric of the etheric country have a material core, of which the earth is a local example?

Am I material? Is love between men and women material? Is the inspiration of an artist material? Is the appreciation of music material? The answer to these questions depends on what you call material. If you mean is it real, does it possess reality, then I say, Yes, for spirit is the greatest reality of life, and that which you call material, the world of matter—is but the shell which surrounds the reality.

Is the etheric country immersed in the electro-magnetic or in the gravitational field of the denser core of material matter so that both travel through space together, with the motion of the earth and the motion of the sun, towards the constellation of Hercules?

We are not affected in the world of spirit by the earth's rotation, for we do not have day and night. Our energy is not derived from that sun whose rays give life to your world. Gravity only applies to things of matter, not to things of spirit. It does not embrace the laws of the spirit.

What is the limit to speed of travel by spirits?

We have no limitation of time or space in our travels. To those who are experienced in spirit life there are no limitations. We can travel to any part of your world of matter with the rapidity of thought, which to us is our great reality. Those who dwell in any grade are limited in their travelling to that grade. They cannot exceed it. They cannot travel higher in the realms of spirit than the unfolding of their character has reached. That is their limitation. But that is the limitation of spirit in spirit life.

Are there separate spirit worlds connected with all inhabited planets?

That which you call the spirit world is but the spiritual expression of the universe, which embraces all life expressed in all planes.

Is there only one spirit world?

Yes, but it has an infinite number of expressions, and life on planets other than earth is embraced as well as your world of matter, because they have their spiritual expression as well as their physical expression.

Are the divisions separated in a geographical sense?

Not geographically, but in the mental scale, which is to some extent conditioned by its physical expression.

Do you mean that the divisions are made in the same way as the divisions between the spheres we know?

Yes. In the world of spirit there are differences for a time until there is the evolution beyond that which is conditioned by a physical life.

Will one be able to recognize, after death, one's child who died when very young?

Yes, because he will be shown the child as he knew it. They always forget that the child will know the parent, for the child has been watching over him all the time and will be the first to greet him when he comes to my world.

How is an inflicter of capital punishment—such as a hangman or the operator of an electric chair—judged when he reaches the spirit world?

If he knows it is wrong, he will pay the penalty for sinning with knowledge. If he does not know it is wrong, then there will be no punishment.

Shall we, after we pass on, be punished for having eaten animal food?

When you have reached that stage in your evolution when you know it is not right to eat the lesser creation of the Great Spirit, then you inflict on yourself a punishment for doing that which you know to be wrong. If you have not reached that stage of evolution, then your soul is not yet aware that it is wrong and there will be no punishment. Always there is a price to be paid for knowledge. That price is responsibility.

PROBLEMS OF COMMUNICATION

Experienced Spiritualists, who know something of the problems of communication, are often amazed that the spirit world ever succeeds in breaking down all the barriers and transmitting its message. So successfully has Silver Birch evolved his system of control that he claims to transmit through his medium the totality of his thought, though he admits that the subconscious mind of the instrument sometimes interferes with the actual words used.

This chapter will give some idea of the work necessary on the Other Side before a medium and the guide are suitably trained.

I AM limited, not only by my medium's vocabulary, but by the state of his soul evolution, because that limits the amount of myself that I can express. As his soul evolves, so I will be able to allow that part of me which is not expressed to express itself.

I can always get through, not the words, but the totality of my thought, because I have learned now where to find the words in his brain. I can get through all the ideas that I have before I come here.

When I began to speak through him, in the early days of his mediumship, the trouble was this, that when I sought to find one word in his brain, that immediately released another word that was linked with it. I had to learn how to control all the nerve centres and, in particular, those of his brain, so that only the right word was used. I do not say that I can eliminate the whole of the medium, because his words can sometimes tinge, in a little way, my ideas. But they cannot rob the idea of what it is I try to express.

Your Western minds are so different from ours. It takes us Indian spirits years to learn to manifest through them properly. We are trained with Westerners, and then, when we have learned sufficient, we experiment with the spirit bodies of mediumistic people while they are asleep. At last we are able to entrance mediums and speak through them, but it is only after very long training.

You do not realize how complicated your bodies are, until you try to use somebody else's. You have to make the heart beat, the blood flow and the lungs contract and expand. You have to keep all the nerve centres fed with the right impulses. You must cut off the stream from the medium's own subconscious mind, and feed your own ideas all the time. It is not very easy.

You have to do all that consciously, every time you speak, at first. That is what development means. In the same way, when you were a baby, you had to learn to put one foot before the other in order to walk. Now, you do not have to think about it. When I first learned to control a medium, I had to do it step by step. Now I do it automatically.

When a medium is controlled by a spirit who has recently passed on, the spirit does not have to do all that before he can speak. All he has to do is to impress his thoughts on the medium's subconscious mind. But even that takes a lot of practice, and we practise on people in our own world. It is not an easy thing. It is much easier to talk through a trumpet, once all the power is properly moulded, than to talk properly through a medium and to get your own thoughts through.

When you get hold of the subconscious, it is already trained through many years to think in certain directions, to express itself in certain ways, to use certain ideas. We strive to bring our own thoughts and ideas and words, so as to make new tracks in the subconscious mind to get our own message through.

If we use ideas that are similar to those that are already there, they get diverted to the well-worn tracks in the subconscious. It is like a gramophone record. If you put the needle on the track, it follows that track round and round. If you want to get your own message through, you must make a new track.

When I come to this room, I come right through the wall, because it is not physical to my vibration. When I am in the medium's aura, it becomes a solid wall to me, because then I register on his vibrations. The medium's aura is my prison now and I am limited by his physical senses.

I have to slacken my vibrations. He has to quicken his. It took me fifteen years to learn.

I cannot see in the dark when I am in the medium's aura. I am limited by his body. I had to learn how to use all the things the medium had to learn when he was a child. It is not worth learning how to use his legs, though, because I never use them. I only want to know how to use his brain and his hands.

When I am in control and repeat a message from another spirit, I am not using the medium's ears then, but my own. It is all a question of his aura and mine. I have an aura that is not so dense as the medium's, and into my aura other spirits can sometimes impinge their thoughts, even when I am in the medium's aura. You can talk to someone on the telephone and also talk to someone in the same room. It is two different vibrations. You cannot do both things together, but they break into each other.

Although Silver Birch can get through his medium the totality of his thought, he is still unable to express the fullness of the inspiration that is given to him:

YOUR world of matter is so slow and thick. It is so ponderous and heavy that the inspiration is lost in transmission, in the endeavour to slow down the higher and more subtle vibrations of spirit. Yours is a dark, clammy world compared with the world of light where I live.

You have not seen the sun in the full radiance of its dazzling splendour. You have seen but the pale imitation. Just as the moon reflects the shadow of the sun, so the sun that you behold is but a pale reflection of our sun.

When I come to your world I am like a bird that is imprisoned within a cage, and when I leave it I am like a bird joyfully released to wing its way through boundless space. What you call death is the opening of the cage and the release of the bird from its prison.

When you ask me to give you a message, I put myself in touch with the vibrations which supply me with the messages for you—I am only a mouthpiece—and it is transmitted to me. When conditions are perfect, I catch all that is shown easily. If there is any difficulty, sometimes caused by disturbances near the séance room, then confusion is created. Suddenly there is a snap of the lines and quickly the message has to be transferred to another message, and that means starting on a new line of vibration.

Sometimes, when I transmit personal messages, I hear what is said and repeat it syllable by syllable, because it is on the same vibration as I am when I speak through the medium. But when I become the instrument for teaching, that is not the same vibration for there is another aspect of consciousness to be used. I have to be impressed with symbols, visions, pictures, intuitions, very similarly to the way in which mediums in your world are impressed by us. I have to express a higher consciousness than that you know as Silver Birch.

When an artist is inspired, he then responds to a vibration which is not the one to which he responds normally. In that state, he is the recipient of a power which enables him to translate visions on to the canvas, but when the inspiration departs he cannot do that. When I strive to give you some of the truths of the laws of the spirit, then I have to express myself in that part of my consciousness which can be touched by the higher powers, so that they can fill me and use me as their instrument.

* * * * *

Questions and Answers:

DOES a guide enter the body of a medium in order to speak?

No, not always. In most cases he works through the aura of the medium.

Does the guide utilize the vocal organs of the medium?

Sometimes. I am using this medium's vocal organs now. If I desired, I could build my own, but that is waste of power. I take control of the subconscious part of the medium, which gives me control over all his bodily organs. I displace his will—which he has agreed I should do—and, for the time being, I am in charge of his body. When I have done my work I retire from his aura and his consciousness returns to pick up the threads once again.

Do you have to displace the medium's spirit body?

Sometimes I do, but it is always connected with his earthly body.

Do precautions have to be taken before a séance is held, to exclude entities who operate forces that would defeat the work?

Yes. The great precaution is to have love in your hearts and in your souls. Then only those who are filled with love can come near you.

Are any preparations made on the Other Side before a séance takes place?

Yes, always we have to make the way clear. We have to harmonize our circles with yours. We have to prepare the way. We have to mix all the elements to get the best results. We work in highly-organized bands for that purpose.

Is it beneficial for a medium to read and study and gain more knowledge from books, or is it better to sit for mediumship relying on his own endeavours and confidence?

It depends on the psychic faculty which is to be developed. I do not agree with those who say that mediums should remain in ignorance of the knowledge that others have gained. I believe always that knowledge is to be preferred to ignorance and I would say—though, of course, I speak only for myself—that it is better for you, as a rule, to have knowledge by study, which only means the experiences of others who have trod your path before, than to work in ignorance.

Is it necessary to live a spiritual life in order to become a good psychic?

The better the life you live, the greater the instrument you become for the Great Spirit, for the higher your life, the more the Great Spirit that is within you is expressing itself. Your soul, as it unfolds through the expression of the life which you live, makes you a greater instrument always.

Would it be correct to say that, however good a medium may be, he would be better still if he were more advanced spiritually?

Always. The higher the life, the greater the mediumship. There is nothing worth while to be achieved unless you are prepared to sacrifice. Isn't that the lesson that all of us who return to your world have had to learn?

How do we become receptive to the influence of those who have passed on?

Those you love and who love you are never lost to you. They do not wander outside the radius of their love, for where their love is there they are. They do not leave you. Sometimes they are closer than at others. Sometimes they can impinge their influence on you. Sometimes you are more receptive. Sometimes you allow yourselves to be mentally enveloped with thoughts of fear, worry and anxiety, and you create a wall which makes it harder for them to get near you. Sometimes you are sad and shed tears, and wash your loved ones away. If you would be calm and peaceful, full of brightness, hope, trust, faith and confidence, you would always feel their presence.

We strive to get as close as we can, but our proximity is dependent upon your atmosphere, your growth, your evolution. We cannot reach those whose souls are so dead to the things of the spirit that we have no point of contact. Where there is an awareness, an understanding, a quickening of the soul, there we can make contact and forge a link and make a bond of unity. It does not always mean that the people we are able to contact are Spiritualists. That does not matter, so long as they have knowledge and understanding of spiritual things. Try to make yourselves more receptive, to be calm, and we will draw close. Do not have fear, worry or distress, for those things create a fog which it is hard for us to penetrate.

When we send our thoughts to our loved ones who have passed on, do they always receive them?

It is not possible to give a straightforward "Yes" or "No," because it depends upon the evolution of the soul. If the one who has passed into my world is on the same mental and spiritual plane as the one in your world, then he will receive the thoughts, but if the two are so far removed from one another that they are on different planes, then the one who has passed on will not receive the thoughts.

If we think too much of those who have passed on, does it hinder them in their progress?

You, who live in the world of matter, have no power to prevent the progress of us who live in the world of spirit. Our progress depends entirely upon our actions, not upon yours.

How can a person become a medium and a clairvoyant?

Every child of matter that seeks to serve the Great Spirit is a medium for the Great Spirit. Am I to say how he can evolve his soul? Has it not been told you so many times? Tell him to love his neighbour as himself. Tell him to serve, tell him to seek to uplift, tell him to do everything which will express the Great Spirit within him. That is the highest phase of mediumship. I cannot tell him how to become clairvoyant, but I can tell him how to open the eyes of his soul so that the light of the Great Spirit can reach him. That is by the same method.

Do you believe good is achieved by mystics who cut themselves off from the world and meditate in solitude?

That all depends on what is meant by "good." It may be that by withdrawing from the world of matter it can help to unfold the powers of the spirit. To that extent it is good. But to me it is greater to be in the world yet not of the world, serving the world by the powers that the Great Spirit has given you, after you have unfolded them yourselves through striving, through effort, through development.

Is it true then that by solitude good can only be done to oneself?

The greatest good is when you forget yourself in the service of others. It is not wrong to develop your powers. It is better to develop them so that when they are developed they can be used in the service of the children of the Great Spirit.

What advice can you give to one who wishes to start a home circle?

You must tell him to have plenty of patience, to be prepared for constant sittings before the power of the spirit can express itself. He should choose a group who blend in harmony, where there is no mental friction, where all can unite with a common interest.

They should meet once a week at the same time, for an hour or perhaps just a little longer, begin with prayer and then be passive. But each, beforehand, should search his own heart and ask the motive, the desire, what it is he hopes to achieve.

If the motive be for service, then let them continue. If it be the desire to play with toys, that is not enough. But if they wish to come together in one place, all of one accord, to enable the power of the spirit to reveal itself, then those who are psychically in tune will be touched by that power and gradually it will reveal itself.

Our aim is not to please the sensation-seeker who desires some new thrill for his jaded being, but to uplift mankind and make it find once again those inherent powers almost lost through lack of usage.

BEHIND THE SCENES AT SÉANCES

Silver Birch here tells of the organization necessary on the Other Side for physical manifestations. The circle had the phenomena of the direct voice and materializations, but these were lost for a time when the circle was reconstructed.

THERE have been at work here a band of spirits. They are of all classes. There are some who come from nearer the planes of matter, because they can assist in the material reactions and provide the things that are wanted by those who arrange the power. That is at one end.

At the other end there are those bright ones who are the shining messengers of the Great Spirit. They have been here, not only when you have been here, but also when you have been asleep. They have gone on with their work. They have all given up the right to enjoy whatever there is in our world for them to have, because they have promised to try to bring into operation in your world some of the laws of the Great Spirit, which as yet operate only as a glimmer of light in a world of darkness.

They have done that because they see here a place where there can be a great temple—great, not because of its size or its height or breadth, but because from here can be spread the light, so that darkness will be dispelled by the light of truth. From circles such as this, your world will get new strength. It will learn that selfishness, injustice, intolerance and all such things must be swept away, because they are contrary to the laws of the Great Spirit.

This work goes on and on because it is part of the work of

the Great Spirit. You have all been chosen because you all have a different experience. These experiences can be blended to form a perfect circle of love, harmony and goodwill, which will enable a temple of light to be built.

The work you do is a mighty work. You are building a temple of the Great Spirit. Sometimes you catch a glimpse of what is happening. Sometimes you are left in the dark, and you begin to puzzle and wonder because you do not understand. But remember that not one moment passes but that we are at work, each one of us, trying to do all we can to bring light into a world of darkness.

The improvement of the direct voice is all a question of trial and effort. You cannot tell until they get through how much they can manage. It is really a great privilege for each of you to witness the growth from the beginning and see the unfoldment every time you sit. It is all a question of vibration. It depends on how much comes through. You only hear the parts that are manifested. The unmanifested parts you do not realize. The great trouble is that there are so many who are anxious to come through.

They all want, at any cost, just to speak a few words. They plead: "Just let me say one word. It will make me so happy." And so they try.

But all the time we go on building and storing and experimenting. Day after day and night after night, people come and work here in preparation for your sittings.

When you want to speak to someone on the telephone, you do not see all the people who had to make it. You only see the hole in which you talk—that is, if you can see holes. And the man you talk to picks up a hole and listens. But between the two holes a lot of work has to be done. It is the same with us. You have a hole and we have a hole, but between them there is a lot of work.

The rays that are used by the spirit helpers at the circle to produce the phenomena are rays of energy which defy all your instruments to register. Only the subtle link of the spirit and the development of the spirit can enable you to be tuned in to them. That is why the chemists on our side are always busy. Although the rays are so powerful, they are not dangerous to you, because you are tuned in to them. That is part of the work. All the time, your spirit bodies are becoming more attuned to the rays, which are visible to us but are unseen and unfelt by you.

There are as many as five thousand spirit people here to-night. There are not only those you knew on earth, and those who are interested in the circle. There are those we bring to hear you talk, because they do not think that it is possible.

Others are brought here so that they can learn how we come through to your world of matter, so that they can use other mediums in other parts of the world. There is a great missionary work, not only for your world but for our world too, for we do not sacrifice any time or power. The great lesson that those in my world have to learn is how to use spirit power in order to impress your minds. The great value of an understanding of these laws is that your minds become accessible. You do not realize how, unknown to yourselves, you are all the recipients of inspiration from the world of spirit.

There are many in your world who are counted as great scientists, great inventors and great teachers. They are only the vehicles of intelligences from my world. It does not matter so long as the truth or the discovery is made known. Who receives the credit is of no account.

We do not work alone in our world, for co-operation is the Law. We form groups, which make, as far as possible, a perfect whole—a mixture of all the qualities most necessary for the work that the group has to do. Then one becomes the mouthpiece for the whole group. I am the mouthpiece of the band with whom I work. It is easier when people work together than when one works by himself. The work that is achieved is the result of the cumulative mind of the group.

The more successful the work, the more the individualities of the band have been merged in perfection, in the same way that the more successful the medium is, the more successful is the merging between the guide and the medium. Otherwise, there would be friction and disharmony.

It is the same as in your world, where each has his allotted task to perform. If the organizer is clever, then he gives to each one just that task for which he is fitted, and then you get the best results. You have an orchestra, each one playing a different instrument, but when they play in harmony then you get a perfect combination. If the smallest of the band strikes the wrong note, then it creates disharmony among even the best players. Co-operation is the law.

* * * * *

Questions and Answers:

IN the production of psychic phenomena, do you make use of materials in the room as well as of the psychic powers of the sitters?

Yes, we make use of the carpet, the curtains, books, even of the furniture. We who are not encased in matter have to use matter, and we obtain it to some extent from the actual substances that are here. We take a little from everything so as not to destroy things. Otherwise, you would find your furniture falling to pieces.

Is that why sometimes in materialization séance-rooms the curtains, say, wear out quickly?

Yes, that is the reason. But we are very careful. Sometimes colour is taken from material things in order to provide the colours used in materializations. When you know more about our work you will learn that nothing is wasted. But the greatest power of all is the power that comes from within each one of you. That is the greatest ingredient.

Mediums must develop not only the powers of their mediumship, but also the powers of their spirit. You must learn that the power of the medium's own spirit raises the quality of the ectoplasm. It is not wood or clay with which we are dealing, but the essence of life as contained in the medium. All the thoughts and character and mentality of the medium go into the ectoplasm.

Is materialization a high or low form of mediumship, and is this form of mediumship advisable?

Anything which brings to one soul happiness or knowledge of the laws of the spirit has served its purpose. Do not think in terms of high or low. Think in terms of service to those who need it.

WHEN NOTHING HAPPENS—

When no phenomena occur, sitters are apt to think they are wasting their time. To these people, the words of Silver Birch, when the circle has been waiting for physical manifestations to be resumed, will be an encouragement:

NO time that is spent in the desire for spiritual attainment is ever wasted. You wait very patiently, I know, but I want you to realize that great progress continues all the time. The bonds of unity between us are being strengthened and there is a quickening in the perceptions of your own soul powers. Growth, unfoldment and evolution are taking place all the time.

The greater manifestations of the spirit are not in their outward expression, but in the quickening of the inner response, in the closer union between the unfolding spirit and the powers which seek to use it.

Whether the manifestation of the spirit is seen or heard does not matter very much. What is more important is the unfolding of your own souls' power, for, as you sit here week after week, so you are attuning yourselves to higher vibrations and becoming more accessible to the wisdom of the ages, which is always waiting to pour itself down into your world of matter, to obey the law of service. But it must find instruments attuned to its vibrations.

And, as your souls unfold and you rise higher and higher in the scale of vibrations, so you come into closer touch with higher and greater spiritual forces, that are not seen or heard but which belong to the eternal realities of the spirit. That is the reality of your lives. So much of your time is spent in chasing the shadows, in trying to capture the illusion, in trying to secure the ephemeral. In silence, in harmony and in love, your souls unfold all the time. Though it may be slow, it is sure and certain.

The Great Spirit that is within each one of you unfolds and evolves, and you are able to express more and more of your divinity, because you have all met together in one place and with one accord. The Nazarene told you, many years ago, that, where two or three are gathered together, there is the Great Spirit to pour down His blessing. We teach the same truth, but they reject us.

Truths do not change. Men's minds change, but truth is constant because it is based upon knowledge, and knowledge comes from the Great Spirit. He is the centre and the source of all inspiration. It is all so simple and so easy to understand, but your world has made it so very difficult.

Because we have met we are enabled to make stronger the links between all of us. There are many spirits who come here who are not known to you, whom you do not greet by name, who come to render service and seek only to serve, who ask for no mention and no reward.

They see here a means of bringing knowledge, of helping truth to advance, of helping to break down all things that are wrong and of helping to drive away sorrow and superstition, to make the light spread further and further, to stop pain, misery and suffering, and to bring happiness, peace and welfare.

That is the work that you are all helping to do. If, sometimes, it seems that you get no results, I ask you to remember that to come here and give us this one hour, with your aspirations to serve, helps to build the temple of the spirit all the time.

Every moment that you sit here, with your hearts attuned to the Great Spirit, is not wasted. With all the power that accumulates when you meet in harmony and love, you are helping to build a great bridge. Over that bridge there will come from my world to yours many who will be able to bring to the world of matter a new light, a new strength, and a new hope. Will you always remember that? While we laugh and joke, behind it all there is a great purpose.

That purpose is that the laws of the Great Spirit shall be able, through each one of you, to operate more fully in the world of matter. To that purpose each one of you has given yourself. The more you can have this common purpose and desire to receive the Great Spirit, the more you will be able to bring His power into your midst.

* * * * *

Questions and Answers:

DO you think laughter at séances is beneficial to results?

The happier you are in your soul, the nearer you are to the Great Spirit. Remember you are the Great Spirit and nothing in your world of matter can touch you. I have sought to teach you that for a long time. As long as you are worried by the things of matter, you will not learn the lesson.

I do not say disregard the things of matter, because you express yourself in the material world, and you have responsibilities to that world. But do not forget you are the Great Spirit and the Great Spirit is you. The power which belongs to the Great Spirit, which belongs to you, can raise you triumphant over all matter.

It is a power which, properly understood, can enable you to resist all evil, to overcome all sickness and to fight every obstacle. But few of you use it. You were taught about it many years ago by the Nazarene, who said, "The kingdom of heaven is within."

Are not some of the best types of mediumship unsensational and unrecognized by the outer world?

I do not think in terms of high or low. Greater or lesser service, that is what counts to me. You must unfold the gifts of the spirit, so that you can give the greatest service to the greatest number of people. In order to do that you must come before your world when you are ready.

It is sometimes necessary for mediumship to be confined to a few, because the power is not strong enough to stand the gaze of those who are outside the confines of the circle, but the whole purpose of mediumship is to enable the world of spirit to deliver its message to the world of matter. The more people that can be reached, the greater is the service that is being accomplished.

I know nothing and care nothing about sensation. I am only interested in service, in giving strength to the weary and hope to those who have lost their faith, in giving a new comfort to those who are distressed in mind, in soul and in body.

Why is it that automatic writing, of all psychic exercises, seems to be the least reliable?

It all depends on the mediums. If they are not developed, they cannot distinguish between the thoughts which they pick up from your world and the thoughts which come to them from ours. That is a matter of development, for as the mediumship unfolds so it begins to reject the impressions of your world and becomes more susceptible to the influence of our world. You must not blame us because your instruments are not developed. We can only work with the material that you give us.

When spirits who have left the astral plane communicate with the earth, do they have to come down to the astral plane in order to do so?

Oh, no. They can always find others through whom their message can be transmitted. They can always use instruments, but they would have to be evolved not only beyond the astral but much more than that. It must not be supposed that only those in the astral, which is the next stage beyond the physical, can communicate with your world of matter, for that is not so. For many spheres or states beyond that it is possible to have direct communication, always depending on your finding an instrument in the world of matter capable o receiving your vibrations.

We are told that the extent of our knowledge in spiritual matters is governed by our capacity to receive. Is it wise, therefore, for people who are spiritually unprepared to seek evidence through mediums?

Evidence has nothing to do with the growth of the soul. Your ability to receive according to your capacity means how far can you reach out to the planes of spirit to receive truth? How far has your soul evolved so that it can understand truth? That must not be confused with the search for evidence. They do not go hand in hand. There are some who have evidence that life is continuous, but whose souls have not yet been touched by the spirit.

WHAT OCCURS IN SLEEP

How many people remember, on awakening, their experiences during sleep? It seems natural that, if we live in the spirit world while the physical body is at rest, we would remember something of that life when we returned to physical consciousness. Silver Birch here tells why a memory of that other life is so seldom registered on our physical brains:

YOUR world of matter makes it difficult for you to remember in the smaller consciousness what takes place in the larger. You will not begin to live until you have died.

Sometimes, in your world, when the spirit rises and effects for a time close union with those who seek to inspire it from my world and you are at one, then you catch for a brief, fleeting moment the happiness that belongs to a world that is supernal.

Practically everybody visits my world during sleep, for it is part of the preparation made by the Great Spirit to accustom the spirit body to its future habitation, so that when the final separation is made there will be no shock and the newly-arrived spirit will gradually accustom itself to its surroundings as memories stir within it, just as you remember gradually when you return to the scenes of your childhood.

The degree of spirit which can be reached is dependent upon the state of the soul evolution. All can travel in spirit, but some are limited in their range.

Some people travel in sleep to the darker spheres of the spirit world, either because that corresponds with their own soul-state or because it is the action of their own free will as they desire to be used in service.

There are many in my world who can be helped by bringing to them the spiritual bodies of those who are in your world. You will find it in the Bible, where it tells how the Nazarene descended into what they called hell. That was not during the sleep-state, but it is the same law.

It is possible to train oneself to remember the experiences during sleep, but it requires concentrated effort because you will have to train the consciousness to register its impressions on the brain cells. That would be easier for some than for others. It depends on how closely the two bodies are knit. Those who find it easiest to remember are those who would make the best mental mediums.

* * * * *

Questions and Answers:

HOW can dreams be accounted for? Some of them can scarcely be accepted as memories of spirit travels.

There are dreams and dreams. Some of them are capable of physical explanation, as they are only the reflex action of a brain which is hushed for a while. Some of them are caused by the food you eat. But beyond all these, there are the dreams which are the memories of your experiences in our world, which you retain in very fragmentary form. The reason why your dreams are often distorted is that when you come to the planes of spirit you are freed from the restrictions of earth and, in the effort to remember spirit experiences in earthly limitations, you get distortion.

Does the communicating spirit know whether he has registered on our consciousness in sleep state?

No, not always. We do not always know at séances, at the time, how much is transmitted. It is often the same when impressing people.

If, during sleep, we frequently meet our guides, why is it that such meetings are so rarely referred to in séance messages?

They are. The questioner will know about them one day, for they are registered in his soul. Even if he cannot recall that memory now through the cells of his brain, one day he will be able to bring it to the surface. You know, things are true whether you know of them or not.

If our spirits leave the physical body during sleep and the body is left, as it were, untenanted, what is there to prevent some wandering earth-bound spirit from possessing or obsessing it? Is any spirit guide "on duty" to guard it against mal-occupation?

What prevents this happening is the natural law that you cannot be obsessed by undeveloped spirits unless you are in a condition to be obsessed. The spirit is not *in* the body, for the spirit does not belong to the same rate of vibration as the body. You—the real you—are not inside the body. You are not tucked in between your heart and your lungs. You are consciousness expressing itself through the earthly machinery of your physical body.

All that happens when you sleep is that the consciousness, instead of expressing itself through the physical body, expresses itself through the spirit body and, because of that, it is expressing itself in the planes of spirit. There is no question of another coming in. It is not as if you have opened the door of your body and someone walks into the body and shuts the door. It is not like that at all. It is that the consciousness, still in charge of the body, expresses itself on another plane and returns as soon as it is time for it once more to associate itself with the physical body.

Does that mean that when a person is obsessed, the intruding spirit has received the permission of the spirit of the person obsessed?

No, but the person obsessed has created within himself the

conditions that make obsession possible. It is all a question of the individual. It is the same as when you are filled with a desire for love and service you attract those higher ones who can use you. It is the same law. The law does not work only for good. It works also the other way. All laws which can be used for the greatest service can also be abused, for as high as you can rise so low can you sink. As low as you can fall, so correspondingly can you rise to the heights. It is the same law. It depends on the way you choose to apply yourselves to it.

Are prophetic dreams "transmitted" to the recipient from your side?

Sometimes they are. Sometimes they are prompted by their own loved ones, who try to warn them. At other times, it is the experience of the spirit body itself which, freed from the limitations of earth, is able to glean something of the future and to bring back in the form of a dream a warning of what it has seen ahead in the path of time.

If the spirit leaves the body in sleep, how is the body animated and why does it not cause death?

Because the silver cord is still attached and consciousness remains. Once the silver cord is severed and the connexion between the physical body and the spirit is gone, there is no more animation.

Where is the spirit, or that part which survives after death, when a person is under an anæsthetic?

I do not know. It might be anywhere. It depends on the evolution of the person as to how far it can go and where it goes.

Is there a difference between the state of unconsciousness caused by a brain injury, and unconsciousness in sleep?

Oh, yes. When you are unconscious because of an injury

that is something which interferes with the normal harmony between your spirit and your body. When you sleep, that is the normal thing, for the spirit knows that every night the vibrations of the physical body slow down and the spirit prepares itself by coming to our world. One is the normal part of your experience and the other is an abnormal happening that interferes with your make-up. In one case the spirit leaves the body voluntarily, and in the other it is forced out because the body is unfit for it to function through it.

TO THOSE WHO SERVE

Silver Birch never loses an opportunity to encourage workers for Spiritualism in their task. He has urged on those engaged in India, Sweden, America and other parts of the world, besides those in England. Here are some typical messages, which gave new enthusiasm to the recipients:

To Carl A. Carleson, one of Sweden's best known Spiritualists:

YOU came here tonight in order that you may be refreshed with the power of the spirit; that you may take it away with you into the far-away places, so that the light of the Great White Spirit may spread and be cast into the places where darkness now reigns. I am very happy to greet you and give you the blessing of the world of spirit upon the mission you promised to undertake many years ago.

I am only the mouthpiece of those who send me to do the work of the Great Spirit. Your footsteps have been led for many, many years upon the path that you must tread. The work which is yet to be done is a great and mighty work. In that work which lies before you, the extent of which you cannot visualize, there will be called to your side, from our world, a band of those who know what must be accomplished in your own country.

Often your heart will bleed because of the difficulties that you will meet; because those you expect to welcome the truth will deny it. Often your heart will rejoice because you will be able to carry this new truth to places where it can be of service to the children of the Great White Spirit. But whichever it may be, whether tears of sorrow or the rejoicing of your heart, we want you to know that when your tears flow ours will flow also; when you rejoice in heart, we will rejoice in heart, too.

No difficulty you meet, no obstacle in your path, will be allowed to impede the plans of the Great White Spirit and those who seek to serve Him from your world and ours. When you do not know which way to turn, stop and relax. Ask for that which will sustain you and will carry you forward once more. There is no limit to the help, the power and the inspiration that will come to you if you will have complete trust and faith in us. We will serve you, as we would that you serve others.

To V. D. Rishi and his wife, India's greatest propagandists:

IN the country where you serve, there is as yet only a glimmer of light in a world of darkness. That little point of light is kept burning by those who know that it is the light of the Great Spirit. It is by the service of people like you that the light can grow and grow. As it grows, all ignorance and selfishness will disappear, and in their place will come a new light of service, which is the biggest part of the Great Spirit.

That is a very big work and nothing in the world of matter can prevent those who serve from fulfilling their task. Your country has many hundreds of years of wrong teaching to undo. You are not working single-handed. There are always with you those from our side of life. The power of the spirit is greater than the power of matter. So far, you have never been failed.

You two have been brought together. It is all a part of the Plan, so that together you can work to bring a new light to the many thousands of souls who are still in the darkness of material things. You have been brought to this circle that you may see what can be achieved by harmony. The contact with the spirit that you will get here will not be ended when the sitting is over. You will feel the power that will go with you and will be with you always.

It will lift you up and will help you to fight every battle. It will remain with you and will help you to remove all the stones in your path. It will urge you on when you feel depressed, lift you up when your eyes are cast down. It will bind you with the Great Spirit of all and will make you understand that those who serve may receive impressions from a power that overcomes all the difficulties of earth. Know that you are never alone. Your fights are our fights and your difficulties our difficulties.

May the Great Spirit be with you in your journeys and in your mission. May His light illumine your heart and give you a greater understanding of His purpose. May you feel that power which will sustain and uplift you, and cause your feet to be placed on the pathways which lead to His knowledge. May you feel His arms and His cloak around you, and know that you are guided and protected in all that you seek to do in His service.

Three years later, when Mr. and Mrs. Rishi again visited the circle, Silver Birch said:

THE ties that I made with you when last you came to England have never been broken, and you will go back to your country with enthusiasm and with a new determination. We know how faint the heart becomes when there are so many obstacles to be surmounted. We know all that lies in your path, and we know how you have struggled valiantly to be true to that light which has been given to you, which you have sought to follow in all its truth and beauty.

We realize how human hearts despair at times when it seems that the road is encompassed by the mists of ignorance. Once again it is my joy to remind you of the great task that brings us all together. One of the scribes in your world said: "East is East and West is West, and never the twain shall meet." But they do meet. They meet because we are all of one spirit, and to the Great Spirit there is no East and no West, no North or South. The children make the boundaries; the Great Spirit seeks to weave all the colours into one pattern of harmonious beauty.

You have been richly blessed, for you have chosen the path of service. You and your wife are one, for you serve together and you stand together. The mantle has indeed fallen on you, and it is the mantle of spiritual love that envelops you, that shields you and guards you.

Think not that you are alone, for behind you there is the mighty host of the spirit world. The work that you do will live, and you, who see only failure, do not realize your successes. Somebody has to hack a pathway through the jungle. Do not despair. You go back to your country and blaze once again that trail which will make it easier for others to come after you.

Dr. Carl A. Wickland, famous for his psychic cures of obsession in America, visited the circle a few months after the passing of his wife, whose mediumship enabled his work to be done. He was accompanied by his secretary, Mrs. Nelle Watts. To Wickland, Silver Birch said:

I AM happy to greet two faithful workers whose backs have become a little bent with their labours and their service, and who can look back through the years and realize that they have helped many to come out of the darkness of ignorance into the light of truth and understanding.

Your work is done—a great and noble work that will be an inspiration to others. Soon you will put down the torch and others will take it up. The work that you have done will not die. It cannot die. Do not expect your world of matter to recognize truth when it comes in your own generation. The way of the pioneer is always full of difficulty. But the work will live on.

At the end of a life of service you can look back and know that many rejoice because you have lived. You have brought new hope and health and restored life itself to many to whom living had become darkness and despair. You have freed them and you have enabled them to take up the thread of life. You have cast them out of their prison. You have helped those in my world who were ignorant of the great harm that they were doing.

Your world of matter does not understand the links between the two states of life. Just as you can have the heights of inspiration from the realm of spirit by those who are the wisest and the greatest, you also have possession by those who are ignorant. It is the same law of attraction that operates.

You have done a great work and in fighting ignorance you have been spurned by those who could have held the hand of co-operation towards you, but you are in the line of succession of all pioneers who have had to fight for their truth and who have left their truth highly prized because of their labours.

My mission is like yours—to undo all the evil that comes through ignorance and superstition. We offer your world of matter the priceless jewel of knowledge, before which all ignorance must ultimately flee.

Do you realize that, out of those whom you have helped to put their feet on the paths of spiritual progress, there is not one who does not return to you to try to help you as you helped them? They, having received service, strive to render service.

Do not think that you are alone. Do not think that your house is empty. Do not think that your wife has left. She is with you still. She is closer than ever she could be. Even though your eyes may not see and your ears may not hear. her spirit is close to yours.

To delegates from America and elsewhere who had attended the meetings of the International Spiritualist Congress at Glasgow in 1937, and who had been invited, with a few others, to a special seance, Silver Birch said:

THE magnitude of spiritual truth has brought you all together, and you have conferred one with another to try to find a new strength and new courage, to return to your own lands with a new understanding and a new hope.

Your world of matter cannot be silent to the voice of the spirit any longer, for you stand at the cross-roads and a choice has to be made.

Your Churches have failed you; they are bankrupt. Your men of science have failed you; they seek to destroy instead of building. Your philosophers have failed you; theirs is but the empty talk of idle speculation. Your statesmen have failed you; they have not learned the supreme lesson that only through sacrifice can peace come to your world. In his despair, the child of the Great Spirit cries out for guidance.

We remind you of the great trust that is reposed in you, the great responsibility that is yours to bear, for there is One that cannot fail—the Great Spirit of all life. If you will but allow His power to guide you, His wisdom to lead you, His love to sustain you, you will find the solution of all your troubles, for you will all find your selves, the true selves, the greater selves that seek not for glory for themselves alone but only desire to serve.

Your world is full of strife and bitterness, full of discord. It is full of tears and misery and bloodshed. And yet each cries: "Give us peace." I urge you all to remember the potentiality that lies within yourselves. *You* are the Great Spirit, each one of you. His infinite power is latent within you. If you will but call it into being and let it rise to the surface, it will break all the bonds of limitation that stand in the way.

Reveal yourselves in the fullness of its hidden glory. Realize that you are indeed the Great Spirit, with infinite power at your disposal, and you will indeed be the instruments of the new age, which slowly is beginning to dawn over a darkened world. Put not your faith in the world of matter or in those who dwell in that world, no matter how high a place they occupy. Look beyond! Try to catch that inspiration that ever seeks to illumine your lives with its desire to serve.

Go forward! And, though you will find many disappointments and many failures, we will always stand behind you, seeking to enthuse you in your days of difficulty, seeking to give you hope and strength when you are tired, seeking to raise you up when you are cast down. You will never be alone. The Great Spirit will send His ministers to guard you. Some of you will go to far-off places. But the power of the spirit will not disperse. It will go with you, striving always to reveal itself in your lives as you desire to serve.

May the blessing of the Great Spirit go with each one of you, and may you realize how infinite is the love which seeks to hold you in its embrace. May you realize that you are enveloped in the mantle of divine love. May you look beyond the difficulties and the trials and the troubles of the world of matter and raise your faces to the sun, the golden symbol of the Great Spirit.

Fill your hearts with love, your minds with knowledge,

your spirits with a determination to serve. Then the will of the Great Spirit will make itself known through you, and all your hearts will beat in unison with His great heart, and you will be at one with Him. May the Great Spirit bless you all.

OTHER-SIDE VIEW OF WAR

Silver Birch has always been unwavering in his denunciation of war and the taking of life in any circumstances. He has always urged the spreading of peace teaching, as is shown by the following selection from his talks:

WE do not want the spirit world to become once again a hospital for broken souls. Those of us who work amongst you know that you must be prepared to take into your world all that which we try to teach you. We cannot do it for you. We can only see the result of those things you do which are wrong and show you what happens in our world when you do wrong things in yours.

It is because we see the destruction and the harm done that we have to point out the result—there come into the spirit world those who are not yet ready. They are plucked from the tree of life before the fruit is ripe. Why should we have to mend broken souls because you have destroyed the means through which they functioned on earth? Why should we have to give up our progress in order to serve those who only come into our world because you have failed to do your duty?

If we did not love, and if we did not express the love of the Great Spirit, we would not be working amongst the children of earth. You must try to judge us only by the truths we try to teach you. You can never say to us: "That which you teach is wrong; it is against our common sense."

It cannot be right, even for your material world, to justify war. Even in things of matter, it leads only to destruction.

It cannot be right for our world, because you interfere with the operation of the law. How dare the children of earth interfere with the divine law that the spirit should drop from the body when it is ripe!

You must stand for that which is right. Those who are blind must not be allowed to interfere with the work of the spirit. You do not know how in your world there is at work an organized effort to upset all that which makes for progress, peace and harmony. Your world has to learn not to think in terms of separate peoples, but to realize that all are the children of the Great Spirit. The barriers are made by the children of earth, not by the Great Spirit. He has given to each one of them a part of His spirit and, because of that, they are all parts of Him.

When there is so much work of construction to be done in your world, why is it that even your "wise ones" seek only to destroy? The Great Spirit has given natural laws to regulate all these things. The children must not seek to interfere with the laws. If you do not live within the Law the result can only be destruction and chaos. Have you not seen it already?

I urge each one of you to do what you can to throw all your weight and your work among those who seek to bring the Great Spirit's plan into your world. Do you think the Great Spirit wants blood to be shed? Do you think the Great Spirit wants misery, suffering, unemployment, hungry people, dirty houses, wars? Do you think the Great Spirit wants His children to be denied the bounty He has given? Do you think the Great Spirit wants little children to be denied guidance from their parents because they have been forced into my world?

If you are loyal to that which we try to teach you—only because, like you, we seek to serve the Great Spirit—you will help in this work. It is against the Law of the Great Spirit for any one to try to put an end to the physical life of another spirit.

When the lust to kill is fostered, reason departs. Not only is the Great Spirit within you, but there is also the remnant of your animal evolution. Your progress and your evolution consist in learning to subdue the animal and in allowing the Great Spirit to shine. If you allow the animal side to come out on top, then you have war and strife and killing, but if you allow the Great Spirit to shine, and you seek to serve one another, then you will have peace and harmony and plenty.

You must not divide your world into countries or peoples. You must try to teach that they are all parts of the Great Spirit. They are all His children. Even those who are divided by seas are brothers and sisters in the sight of the Great Spirit of all. Our teaching is simple but true. It is founded on the laws of the Great Spirit. If you seek to build your world, ignoring the Law, you must have chaos and disorder. You become bankrupt.

There will be many wars in your world of matter unless great efforts and sacrifices are made. You have sown the seeds and you must reap what you have sown, for you cannot cheat the law of cause and effect. You cannot sow bloodshed and reap peace. You cannot sow the desire for material power and then expect to escape the consequences. Sow love, and love will come. Sow peace, and peace will arise. Sow seeds of service everywhere and the world will be filled with service. These are the simple truths of the Great Spirit. They are so simple that they confound the "wise ones" of your world.

Questions and Answers:

DID not any good at all come out of the sacrifices of those who "died" in the War?

I can see none. Your world of matter is nearer chaos today, and is more filled with destruction, than it was when your "Great War" began.

Can so much heroism be spent in vain? Is there no spiritual repercussion?

There is on the part of the individuals who made the sacrifice, because their motive was good. But do not forget that your world has betrayed them. It has made their sacrifice pointless, because it has continued in its materialism.

Is it of any use that Armistice-services should go on, year after year?

It is better to remember those you call dead for two minutes than not to think of them at all. But I do not see what good can come when you celebrate the Armistice with a display of military might, with rifles and bayonets, with soldiers, with the firing of maroons and with all that comes with war. Could you not have an Armistice that was a spiritual service?

Are you in favour of the continuance of Spiritualist services of remembrance on that date?

Wherever truth is expressed good is done, if speeches are given as an incentive to service. Vain speeches that lead to nothing are valueless. It is not sufficient to have speeches, and for audiences to be smugly satisfied with the feeling that they are in favour of peace. I want them active. I want them serving. I want them uplifting the weak. I want them healing the sick. I want them comforting the mourner. I want them sheltering the homeless. I want them to put an end to all the abuses that are a blot on your world of matter. Only through service can peace come. It will not come until all are imbued with the ideals of service, until all practise service. For nineteen years they have been holding Armistices, and today the Armistice is but a short break in the preparations for war.

Do you agree with the Pacifist movement?

I belong to no party. I wear no label. I see service, motive. Do not be confused with titles. Ask what is the aim, what is the desire, because there are men of honesty and good intent even in opposing camps. The teaching that we have to give you is very simple, but it requires courage to put it into practice. Whenever a start is made, whenever there is the determination that comes with knowledge of the spirit and the truths of the spirit, whenever service and not selfishness is applied to all the affairs of every-day life in the world of matter, then you will have peace and concord in your world.

It will not come through any party, but through the children of the Great Spirit who, realizing these things are true, apply them in their lives, in their politics, in their factories, in their governments, in their international transactions. We can enunciate principles that we know are founded on truth, and tell you with certainty that their application will bring results. You are in the realm of matter. Yours is the responsibility. We can only strive to guide you, with all our love and helpfulness, and co-operate with you whenever your feet are on the right paths.

Would it not be folly for Great Britain to refrain from arming in view of the undoubted fact that other great powers of Europe are armed to the teeth?

Have I not already said so many times that you think in terms of one country and one people while I think in terms of the Great Spirit and all His children? I tell you that you will not find peace by making machines of destruction. You find peace when there is a desire for peace and when all people live by the law of love and service. I do not think only of one country and one race of people. I think of all peoples as one, as part of the Great Spirit. They are all His children. Until you apply His laws to your world of matter, you will have war and destruction, pestilence, havoc, chaos and bankruptcy all over again.

The following questions were asked in reference to the Italian invasion of Abyssinia:

Does the spirit world agree with sanctions?

You know my views. Life belongs to the Great Spirit, not to His children. They must not shorten life. That is against the Law. And, if they do that, they must pay the price.

But in this case the motive would be good, for it would be an attempt to stop the war.

If you sow the seeds of might, then out of those seeds there can only come more might. Have you not been told before by those who are your earthly counsellors that it was a war to end war?

Do you think we should let a bully kill innocent people?

You want us to pronounce a verdict on half-way happenings, but we deal with eternal principles. If the eternal principles had been applied in the beginning, then you would not have your present difficulties. Because you have reached difficulties, you say to us: Shall we apply some measure which may, for the moment, remedy the evil which has accrued? Only eternal principles can procure eternal peace.

Should we not support the League of Nations?

Is there a desire among those who are counsellors of nations for peace? Is peace in their hearts and in their souls? Are they determined to abide by the eternal principles of the laws of the

Great Spirit, or do they merely seek to stop that which might become a menace to their own countries? Do they not still think in terms of wealth and nation and race, instead of in terms of the Great Spirit and His children? We deal with the eternal principles, with the Great Spirit and His laws and their operation. There is no other way.

You may succeed for a time with your half-measures, but out of evil always there will come evil. One day, your world will realize that love can overcome evil because love is the expression of the Great Spirit. When, in the spirit of love, all people seek to solve their problems, then peace will reign in your world. But all desires which are contrary to the law of love will always produce disruption, chaos and bankruptcy. You must strive to deal with roots, for by no other way can you have eternal peace.

Is there not some reason for war in the cosmos?

No. You make wars in your world. We do not make them in ours. But whenever you have the lust to kill, you always attract those who are bound to earth with similar desires.

Silver Birch usually gives a message for Armistice Day. In 1937 it was:

EACH succeeding year makes the futility of this human sacrifice more apparent. Your world will pay for just two minutes of its time a silent tribute in memory of the "glorious dead," and after that they will be forgotten for another year, until they are taken off the shelf and dusted once again.

Their sacrifices were all in vain. They have been crucified for nineteen years. The Great War! Its greatness consisted in the amount of slaughter, wasted slaughter. The Great War, that was to end all war! How hollow, how full of mockery do those words sound!

Do you not consider that those who made every sacrifice that they could make in the world of matter, even to laying down their physical lives, have not spent years in bitter disillusionment? They were cut off in the prime of earthly life. They were sent unprepared into the world of spirit. They passed on cheerfully for an ideal, that your civilization might be saved, and they have been betrayed ever since.

War has not been driven from the face of the earth, for, even as you will pay tribute to the "fallen dead," as you call them, of your last war, there will be no armistice in the East or in Spain, where the killing will continue even without a cessation of two minutes.

Does your world of matter realize that peace can only come from the application of spiritual laws to worldly matters? It is selfishness that brings not only war, with its train of bloodshed, misery and weeping, but chaos, confusion, disaster and bankruptcy.

They must learn that only by substituting service for selfishness can peace come, that the old ideas of materialism and power and desires to aggrandise nations must be swept away and in their place there must reign the desire to live for one another, the stronger to help the weaker, the richer to give to the poorer.

Do not insult those who have been translated to spirit realms with tributes that come from the lips and not from the heart. All other methods have been tried and they have failed you. But not yet has the application of spiritual truths been tried. Unless your world does so, it will continue with war and bloodshed that will, in the end, destroy your much-vaunted civilization.

REINCARNATION

Reincarnation is the most controversial subject among Spiritualists. There is even disagreement about it among the guides. Silver Birch declares reincarnation to be true, but he explains that different portions of consciousness incarnate at different times. Below are some questions he has answered on this subject:

IS it possible for one's consciousness to function in separate portions?

There is a consciousness which is you, of which you in the world of matter are expressing but a tiny portion, and there are portions of that same consciousness which are expressing themselves in other spheres of expression.

Independently?

No, not independently. You and the other expressions are all reflections of one inner spiritual reality. They are parts of a whole and the fragments are expressing themselves as parts of the whole, but through different vehicles of expression, which sometimes coalesce. They are not ignorant of each other within themselves, but only when they first begin to express themselves, until they find a common meeting-place and fit together into the whole once again.

Would it be possible for two of those parts to meet one another and not know?

Try to picture the greater consciousness as a circle, and then realize that there are segments of that circle which are revolving round its centre. Sometimes those segments meet and when they meet there is a recognition of their common oneness. When they finally cease to revolve, the different segments occupy their allotted places and the circle is united and complete.

Is it possible for two parts of the same spirit to communicate with each other?

If it is necessary.

Are sometimes two parts of the same spirit incarnated on earth at the same time?

No, for that would be contrary to the whole purpose. The purpose of the individual is to find experience on all planes of expression and only to return to the same plane when there is something to be achieved by the return.

Would it be true to say that each reflection of the spirit has to work out its own progress, and cannot benefit from the lessons learned by other reflections of the same spirit?

Yes, they are all parts of the one soul which express themselves in different forms. You become increasingly conscious of more and more of yourself.

And there is a point in evolution at which all those different parts are joined?

Yes, in infinity.

Would it be true to say that each of these sections incarnates only once and that, while reincarnation would be true when considering the complete soul, it would be untrue of each section?

It depends on what has to be fulfilled. Only when some special mission has to be performed would the same portion of consciousness incarnate more than once.

What do you mean by different parts of the same consciousness?

It is hard to answer you because you do not understand what living really means. Life to you has expressed itself practically in its lowest forms. You cannot visualize real life, living intensely in a consciousness that is superior to anything which you conceive.

The highest experience of the mystic, the greatest inspiration of the artist, the rapture of the poet—even these are but faint shadows of the reality which we call life in spirit realms. When you cannot appreciate that, because your expression is limited to a world of matter that vibrates slowly, how can I explain to you what consciousness is and how it is able to register itself?

Do you see my difficulty? If you had a measure of comparison it would be easier, but you can only compare light with darkness, sunshine with shadow. You cannot compare the colours of the rainbow with colours that are beyond your means of understanding and appreciation.

Are they different virtues or facets of character that are split?

No, not at all. It is not another facet of the individuality at all. When you ask these questions it is like trying to explain to one who has been blind from birth what the colour of the sky looks like when the sun is shining. You have no standard of comparison.

Does not your explanation of "split" consciousness express the same truth as F. W. H. Myers's declaration regarding "group" souls?

It is really the same thing, except that it is not a grouping of different souls, but a union of the different portions of consciousness returning to complete the whole.

It seems that when the different parts of consciousness are reunited each would lose its own individuality.

Does the stream lose itself when it flows into the mighty ocean, or is the ocean many streams? Does the note of the violin lose itself when it merges into the harmony created by the whole orchestra?

Why does not the spirit world give us proof of reincarnation?

What could be evidence of reincarnation that you could not explain by spirit control? You will only accept it when your consciousness is ready, when it becomes clear to you that it is the Law. That is why there are many in my world who say it does not happen. They say it does not happen because they have not yet reached the stage of consciousness when they know it does happen. Can a mystic explain his mysticism to a man of business? Can an artist explain to those not endowed with his sensitiveness what his inspiration is? He cannot. They are on different mental planes.

Does the soul know when it is about to reincarnate?

The soul knows, but cannot express itself through the mind. The soul, which is the Great Spirit, expresses itself through all eternity, gradually, step by step, and at any stage there is a vast portion still not expressed.

Is it, then, unconsciously done when a soul reincarnates?

It depends on the state of evolution of that soul. There are many souls who know they have incarnated before. There are others who do not. Their souls may know, their consciousness may know, but it may not be known by the mind. You are touching the greatest mysteries of life, and I find it very hard to discover words in your English language to express the things of the spirit.

If life is continual change and evolution, and reincarnation is a fact, how can we be sure of meeting our loved ones when we pass over, and of enjoying the life of bliss with them promised to us?

Love will always know its own, for love is the greatest force in the universe. Love will always attract its beloved and love will always meet its love, for nothing can prevent the union of those who love.

But with reincarnation there will be continual separation. Does that fit in with the idea of eternal bliss?

Your idea of eternal bliss does not fit in with my idea of eternal bliss. The universe and the laws in it are as the Great Spirit made them, not as His children make them. The wise man changes his mind as he faces new facts, because he knows that he cannot alter the facts to please his fancy.

If it is true that we have been through countless lives before this one, why is it that we are not more progressed and ideal than we are?

You can be in the world of matter and be a saint; you can

be in the world of matter and be the lowest of the low. It does not depend upon the earthly plane. It depends on the evolution of the soul.

Have we still an infinite number of suffering and struggling lives to go through in the future, as in the past?

Yes, infinite. Struggle, suffering, through the crucible of pain does the Great Spirit express itself. Suffering tries the Great Spirit. Suffering enables the Great Spirit within to emerge purified, strengthened, refined, even as the gold emerges from the ore by crushing, by refining. Until it has been through these processes, it is not revealed as gold.

If that is so, what is the use of the idea of a heaven after death?

That which you consider heaven today you will not consider heaven tomorrow, for happiness consists in striving, always striving, for the higher and the higher beyond that.

If a soul is reincarnated, does it come back to the same nationality as it functioned in in the last incarnation—Indian to Indian and British to British, for example?

Not necessarily. It will choose that country and that race which is necessary for its new unfoldment.

Does the same thing apply in matters of sex?

Yes. It does not necessarily come back to the same sex that it had before.

Can it be true that we are punished for our sins in another life on earth, as well as having to atone before we can progress in the spirit world? Would God punish us twice for the same sin?

It is not always a question of punishment, but of evolution, of a task to be learned, of another link to be forged in the chain of the soul's education and upliftment. Reincarnation does not always mean that you are to be punished. It often means that there are gaps which have to be filled. Sometimes they are chastening ones, sometimes they are lessons which have not been learned. It does not always mean punishment. You cannot be punished twice. When you have an understanding of the Law you will marvel at its perfection, for it cannot be unevenly weighted on one side. The Law is perfect because the Great Spirit is perfect.

Can you tell of anyone on the Other Side who knows for a certainty that he or she has gone through one or more periods of reincarnation in this world?

Yes. When the soul has evolved to the stage where it is necessary for it to know, it knows. It cannot see the light until its eyes can stand the light. I will not give names, for they would not be evidence. I have said before that all which is true of reincarnation can be "explained" by control. I speak of the laws of the Great Spirit as far as my own understanding reaches. I only speak the truth as I know it. If there are some who do not agree, I do not mind, but I can only speak about the things I know. It does not matter if others do not accept it. When they have lived as long as I have, they may change their minds.

There is a lot of controversy regarding reincarnation. Would it not be wiser to concern ourselves with Survival?

It is better to be in the light than in the dark. It is better to have knowledge than ignorance. It is better to know the laws than not to know the laws. It is better always to search for truth, diligently and patiently, rather than to sit still. It is always better to strive for progress. Survival is not the end. It is only the beginning, for when you understand that you are a part of the Great Spirit and because of that you pass through the avenue of death unharmed and unchanged, that is not the end of all things. That is only the beginning.

FESTIVALS IN THE BEYOND

Every Christmas and Easter, Silver Birch, with many other guides, attends a festival in the inner spheres of the spirit world. At these festivals, the guides exchange views on the work they have done and intend to do, and fresh power and inspiration are obtained to help them through the next phase of their work. At these festivals, too, counsel is taken with Jesus of Nazareth, who occupies an important position in the work of perfecting communication with the Other Side.

I WISH that you could see and hear the Nazarene and feel that great love as he encourages us in our missions, as he expresses his knowledge of all that has been done and urges us to go forward with new strength, with new hope, with new vision and with new purpose. He is not the Nazarene of the Churches—exalted into a deified place—but a great spirit who strives still to serve through many instruments.

For a short time I am in the spheres where I lived for many years, to feel once again that vitalizing power of the spirit, so invigorating in its strength, so beautiful in all its fullness, making you realize what life is when you are able to experience it in the higher realms of spirit. I speak with all humility and with no pride at all . . .

If all the beautiful paintings of the world, all the inspired visions and all the great artistry that you have ever heard of in your world of matter and all the deepest and greatest beauties of nature were all combined into one whole object it would be but a very pale reflection of life in the higher regions.

When the artist is filled with inspiration he realizes that it cannot be expressed with his few pigments, and he longs for the colours that could be blended to produce that richness that has been given to his soul. But there are none, for spiritual truth and beauty exceed material clothing.

How can I describe spiritual exaltation in words? How can I describe the joy of meeting beings who radiate the great light of the Great Spirit, who are full of wisdom and understanding, mercy and tenderness, who know all before you convey it, who know your innermost thoughts, who see the workings of your mind, who know of your successes and failures?

You have not the words for these greater experiences of the soul. The past few months are reviewed, plans are made, our tasks are allotted to us. We are urged and encouraged and enthused and we return to strive to perform our allotted missions. With your help and the power that is ours, we strive to bring the children of the Great Spirit nearer to the Great Spirit than ever they were before.

* * * * *

Questions and Answers:

WHEN you attend the festival in the spheres, do you leave earth geographically or in the sense of withdrawing into a different vibration?

When I leave, I am no longer concerned with the gravitational pull of earth or even its vibrations. I leave behind the astral body through which I manifest to you and resume in the spiritual body which is mine—which is, as it were, "cloaked down" while I talk to you here.

Some portion of my consciousness is left in the astral body, so as to prevent its disintegration, but I withdraw and register more and more of my inner consciousness. That is why I ask for as much time as I can get, for the more time that I can use to get freed from the vibrations of earth, the higher degree of consciousness can I register in the spiritual spheres which I desire to reach.

But I do not succeed in attaining to the consciousness I expressed before I came down to your world of matter. I cannot accomplish in a few days that which took years.

Great sacrifice must be involved in deliberately "cloaking down" the consciousness you knew.

That is so. That is the price I gladly pay to try to serve your world of matter.

It must be the biggest sacrifice of all.

Yes, it is, but there are so many who need so much that I rejoice to give up what I have.

If you could have radiant sunshine—not the pale reflection that you know here—and all the perfection of beauty that is expressed in all art, architecture, poetry, and music, and if you could have developed to the greatest degree the beauteous sights that nature could produce in its most harmonious conditions, and enjoy the congenial companionship of souls with similar tastes and pursuits, and then you were plunged into slime, surrounded by darkness and dreary misery—that is to some extent a comparison with what I have to give up. I say that not to aggrandize myself, for I cheerfully relinquish whatever I have earned if only I can help and serve and bring peace and comfort and hope and help to a few.

Silver Birch explains, in the following answers to questions, why the festivals in the spirit world are at the times of the corresponding festivals on earth:

WHY do you hold your festivals at Christmas and Easter? Have they any relation to the Nazarene?

We held these festivals before the Nazarene came into your

world. They have nothing to do with the story in the Bible. One day you will understand that the world is ruled by rhythm, by cycles which are part of the law of progress. These cycles operate and make themselves felt in your world at certain times in the history of all races.

When I lived in your world there were two festivals which were regarded as important. The Christians took those festivals from us and you now call them Easter and Christmas. Those times had a significance to us, because it was then that we received the greatest communion from the Great White Spirit. You do not yet understand, very much, the influence of the sun. At these times, we held for many days what you call séances. We got at those festivals much inspiration.

So, when it again comes round to the times which all of us regarded as the most important in our lives, we gather together and celebrate those times with those who are our own. This started with the influence of the sun, but that was only a symbol. There is an influence from all life to other life, from all matter to other matter, and from all planets to other planets.

It is all based on natural law, for at Christmas is the birth of the sun. This time is chosen because all of us are associated with races whose religions were founded upon the laws of nature. To us, the festival of the birth of the sun was the greatest of all because it represented the beginning of a new era. It is the end of the cycle, and the new cycle begins.

Because these festivals were held in the world of matter, they are celebrated in the world of spirit. A spiritual meaning has now come out of them and, instead of celebrating the dawn of the new life, we now use it to withdraw from the world of matter to get new power of the spirit so that we can bring new light to your world.

For whom is the festival held?

It is largely for the Indians and for the guides who belong

to the older races. All the Western world is new in comparison with these races, and for those who dwell in the West our festival has no significance.

At Easter, we celebrate the resurrection of all life. It is the symbol of all the worlds rising to join in the prayers of all those who pray that your world shall be resurrected from misery, pain, sorrow, sadness and suffering, resurrected into its fuller life, into its real life, so that sadness and tears shall be abolished, so that misery and starvation shall be done away with, and that empty bellies may be filled.

Your world very much needs resurrection, but slowly the laws of the Great Spirit are beginning to operate as more and more of His children allow themselves to be used for His purpose and as the forces of materialism are being driven away.

I go back, with many others, to the spheres where I really belong, to taste for a very short while the joys of spirit life, such as you cannot understand in your limited expression, to see the faces of those we love, who are our teachers, to imbibe of their wisdom, to partake of their power, to hold counsel with the wisest of the wise, to learn how far we have progressed, and where we have failed, to hear the plans that have been unfolded for the great fight that rages ceaselessly—the fight between good and evil.

We go to receive encouragement, to mix with those others who work near the planes of matter, and then to come back again so that, filled with the joy of service, we may co-operate with you all and bring the power of the spirit into your midst. I wish I could take you with me, to gaze on the faces of those who serve you, so that you could see the radiance of the light that illumines them, so that you might realize who are those whom the Great Spirit has given to be your guides. But you might only be afraid. It is better that you know us not by our names, but that you judge us by the work that we seek to do in your midst. But, most of all, I wish I could take you all to that vast council chamber, where we all meet to learn how we have fared amongst you.

* * * * *

Questions and Answers:

WHY did you choose our Easter for the celebration in the spirit world?

We did not choose your Easter. You chose ours.

Was this festival celebrated all over the world at the same time?

To all our races it was celebrated at the same time. When your world began to make a religion of Christianity, it used the symbols of ancient times, because they were the foundations of all religion.

Do the other religions hold a festival in the spirit world at Easter, as well as the Indian communities?

The festival is celebrated throughout the spheres. Those who are Christians celebrate the arisen Nazarene. We who existed in the world of matter long before the Nazarene trod the earth carry into the world of spirit the symbol of our own religion, and make it an occasion for a great festival. At that festival we can learn the wisdom that has still to be revealed to us. We can sit at the feet of teachers greater than ourselves. We can share with others the knowledge that we have learned.

WHEN SORROW COMES . . .

In this chapter, you will find Silver Birch's views on bereavement, suicide, euthanasia, birth control and cruelty to animals.

While Silver Birch's work is mainly teaching, the need for comfort is always stressed. Following are some remarks to a woman sitter whose husband had recently passed on:

SOON you will begin to understand that the unity of the spirit is greater than the unity of physical things. Your husband is much closer to you now than ever he could be in your world.

The loss of the physical presence is great, only because your world has not progressed beyond the vibration of matter. When it has progressed it will realize that matter is only the shadow. It is because you are in the shadow that you think it is real.

When you are evolved you will be able to distinguish between the light and the shadow caused by the light. The ties of earth do not bind, but the ties of spirit endure for ever.

You must try to understand that what seems to you a great sorrow is part of a plan which will be a great help to many. You must not look at it from a personal view. If, through the experience which comes to you, many can be lifted up, then that helps to develop your spirit. It will be of great help to you when you also come over on this side and join him.

The "dead" do not leave you. They pass through a door into a new life. For them it is a great release. It is not hard for them. Their only sorrows are your sorrows.

In your evolution, you are still more responsive to material vibrations than to the vibrations of spirit. Your spirit friends are very near to you, nearer than they were before they lost their material bodies, but you only respond to the slow vibrations of matter and you cannot pick up the quick vibrations with which they surround you. You are not physical. You are spirits now, who have come into the world of matter to learn the lessons of matter. When you have learned those lessons you go on. If sometimes it is a hard lesson, is it not worth it?

Why do you try to judge eternity by physical things? You cannot measure the sky; you cannot even measure your own world. Yet you want to measure all eternity by the few years that man lives in your world.

WHY SUICIDE IS WRONG

Silver Birch's attitude to suicide is uncompromising. It is absolutely contrary to the Law to curtail one's life on earth. His answer to a question from one who had considered this step prevented her from committing it. The question and the answer were:

IS it ever permissible for a person to pass on by his own act—such as the one who is left of a devoted companionship?

No. You must live your lives according to the Law, for the Law is always perfect in its operation. It is controlled by perfect love and by the Great Spirit, Who is in all things and Who works through all things. You have no right to interfere with the operation of the Law, and if you do you must pay the price for cutting yourself off.

If you force the apple to drop from the tree before it is ripe, then the apple has no sweetness. If you force yourself to go into the next stage of life before your spirit is ready, then you will have to pay the price in the long adjustment that you will have to make. It will also have the effect of causing you to be separated from the ones you love, for you will have made a gulf.

After this answer had been published in "Psychic News", the woman wrote:

I do not know whether you thank Silver Birch for answering questions. But, if so, will you please tender him the gratitude of "The One Left Behind" for so quickly as well as so clearly replying? And tell him that, though bitterly disappointed at his dictum, I will accept his ruling and "carry on" to the best of my ability till I receive my call.

SHOULD DOCTORS END LIFE?

Euthanasia (easy, painless death) has been hotly debated inside and outside the Spiritualist movement. Is it ever permissible for a doctor to cut short a patient's life to end pain, where the illness is considered to be so advanced that recovery is impossible? Apart from the fact that it is never possible to say that a patient will not recover—the almost unbelievable successes in spiritual healing are one objection to euthanasia—Silver Birch maintains that life is sacred.

WHAT have you to say about the plea that doctors should be empowered by law to put an end to the life of one who is suffering without any hope of recovery?

I say that all life belongs to the Great Spirit. When it is time for a body to fall away and the spirit to become emancipated, then, obeying a natural law, it does so.

Do you believe it right to prolong the life of a person by physical means?

Yes.

Even if by prolonging life you prolong their suffering?

Yes. But you forget one thing. When it is time for the soul to be released it goes, and there is nothing that you can do in your world of matter to alter that law.

Would the killing of incurable people bring them more suffering to be worked out on the Other Side or in another life?

No, but it would give a shock to the unready spirit and that shock would affect it. A great deal of adjustment would have to be made which would not otherwise have been necessary.

Have we the power to prolong life?

You try to keep the body alive. That is right. But when the time for the spirit to depart has come, you can do no more.

Are our efforts to prolong life useless, then?

Yes. If, as you say, doctors can keep people alive, why is it that death defeats them?

But patients can be kept alive for a time.

Only if the sick man can respond. You can give oxygen, but only up to a point. When the soul is ready for my world, then there is nothing you can do.

If the time of passing is fixed, and the spirit in normal conditions passes to the next world only when it is ready, why is it that the expectation of life is rising?

Because your world is evolving. It is not the physical that determines the spiritual, but the spiritual that determines the physical.

BIRTH CONTROL

Is it right to attempt to prevent the entry of souls into this world? Silver Birch's remarks on birth control must be taken to refer only to the prevention of birth and must not be read as an implied sanction to abortion—and every "remedy" after conception is an abortion, for the spirit has already contacted matter and the earth life has begun.

WHAT is the spirit world's view of birth control?

You have been given free will and a conscience to distinguish between that which is wrong and that which is right. It always depends on the motive. Say that once. Say it a hundred times. What is your motive? It is that which counts, nothing else.

But does the restriction of births interfere with the Law?

Where there is to be born a spirit through two in your world, it will come through those who will not prevent its entry. The Law is supreme. If it is part of your evolution that through you there is to come into your world a spirit, a new life, then you would not prevent it because you would desire it.

Then, if it was to be, you would want it to happen.

Yes, because you would have reached that stage in evolution where it was necessary that the influence of a new life should be brought into your life.

Is that necessarily a higher evolution?

No, it is not high, it is not low. I must make a distinction between those who seek only to enjoy the lust of the body and to prevent the consequences. With that I do not agree, because the motive is one of lowly selfishness.

But if one had an idea it was not advisable, from the child's point of view, what then?

Is that not the motive? It always depends on the motive.

You cannot cheat the Law. The Law is registered on your soul. Every act, every thought, every idea, every desire is registered for ever on the aura of your soul. It can be read by those who have the eyes of the spirit. The motive of everything you have ever done in your world of matter is known by those who see with the eyes of spirit. Your soul is naked before them.

At what period after conception does a spirit enter the body of a baby?

I know that many will not agree with me, but I say that from the moment the two seeds have become one and there is provided in that very miniature form a vehicle through which a spirit can function, from that moment the spirit starts its earthly career.

If the life of an insane person is a waste of time, in that he is unable to learn anything through physical defects, what is the view of the spirit world regarding sterilization, which would prevent hereditary insanity and would avoid that waste of time?

I cannot, and no one throughout the whole universe can alter the law of life. When a soul is ready to be born into your world of matter, the soul is born. You ask why. I preach reincarnation. That is the reason.

CRUELTY TO ANIMALS

Ignorance is no defence if natural laws are broken. To inflict unnecessary pain, on man or beast, is an infringement of the Law and a good motive is not sufficient to wipe out the bad effect. Below are Silver Birch's replies to questions asked about cruelty to animals:

HOW do you view the ever increasing practice of experiments on living animals, often causing terrible pain to helpless creatures?

Many people on this side are striving to get this unholy thine stopped. Are they helped in any way from the spirit world?

Every soul that desires to serve at once brings to its aid those in my world who will inspire and sustain and bring them new power of the spirit to aid the work they seek to do. It is wrong to administer pain to any of the creatures of the Great Spirit, but you must remember that there are many who do it in ignorance, not realizing the pain that they inflict, only possessed with motives to help their fellow men. But they are still breaking the Law.

But if, as we are often told, only the motive counts, will those people who inflict pain in what they conceive to be service to their fellow men have to pay the penalty for breaking the Law?

The motives may be good, but the principle is unaltered. If one deliberately inflicts pain, knowing it will hurt, that means that the one who does it is conscious of his responsibility. His motives, of course, are good, but he has inflicted pain. All these facts are taken into account, but I cannot agree with the practice of inflicting pain.

Are animals sent to earth to help mankind?

Oh, yes. And mankind is sent to help them.

But is the sole purpose of the animal creation not to be of use to man?

No, that is only part of the work.

Do you believe that vivisection can be right when it is undertaken with a good motive?

No. How can that which is cruel be right? How can that which causes pain, which inflicts torture, be right? It is contrary to all that we teach. It is wrong to experiment on those who are not capable of resisting.

Do you agree that no cure for cancer will ever be found by that method?

Your world cannot produce remedies for the diseases which it has created by living contrary to the laws of the Great Spirit.

There will be found remedies for all your diseases, but they will not be found by experiments on animals.

Why does not the spirit world interfere when it sees so many appalling atrocities committed on animals?

Because the universe is ruled by natural laws.

REPRESSING SPIRITUAL GIFTS

Three important aspects of Spiritualism are explained by Silver Birch in the pages that follow. They are the suppression of psychic faculties, the need for service and spirit guidance.

The development of mediumship has two facets. There is the increased sensitivity, not only to things associated with the spirit world but also to those in this world. There is also the responsibility of mediums to use their gifts for others.

Silver Birch told a sitter who had the gift of psychometry:

YOU have accepted the service of the Great White Spirit by coming into this circle. You have been given the gift of mediumship. Use it.

The power that the Great White Spirit permits in His children must be used for all His other children, and if you do not use it, it works against you. You choke something that belongs to the Great White Spirit, and it always upsets you. You cannot keep it bottled up; it will burst.

You must use the powers you have. I did not make the Law, and I cannot alter it. I am only trying to help you. The laws of the Great White Spirit are there for the use of all His children. The troubles come in your world when the children think they are greater than the Parent and try to upset His laws.

★ ★ ★ ★ ★

To another medium, very discouraged because of the unkindness of other people, which she felt more than most people would, Silver Birch said:

YOU are in the hands of a very great and mighty spirit guide If you have complete trust and faith, all will be well. You are an instrument of the Great Spirit, but you have free will. You all have free will. But I ask you to remember the many who can be rendered service through you. There is a mighty power to be used through you. Trust it to operate. It will sweep away all things that stand in its way.

You are very sensitive. You suffer from all the troubles of a medium. It is the Law. I wish I could take on my shoulders all the pains and sufferings of your world. Listen . . .

Do you think we are happy when we see the children of matter denied bread, when we see hunger and want? Do you think we are happy when we see disease? Do you think we are happy when we see spirits sent out of their bodies by weapons of destruction? Do you think we are blind to the sorrows and suffering in your world? But we know there is only one way to put them right.

It is no use for us to take away the wrongs of your world. Out of your own strength must be born a new world of matter. Those who are sensitive to the world of spirit must pay the price of being sensitive to the sorrows of the world of matter. You cannot have it any other way.

I ask you to turn away from the things of matter and cast your eyes to the sun of the Great Spirit, so that its rays may envelop and enfold you and you may know that nothing can touch the undying spirit that is within the frail body. Circumstances may affect your body here and there, but they cannot touch the gold of the Great Spirit that is within you.

If you are not more sensitive to the things of matter, how can you be sensitive to the far more delicate things of the spirit? Put not your faith in the things you can see, but in the things which are unseen, the things of the Great Spirit, the eternal things.

When I have seen my own medium suffer, and when I have been shown, before, that he is about to suffer, can you not imagine how the tears have flowed from my eyes? I have wished I could take all his burdens on my shoulders. But I know the Law, that only through suffering can the spirit be purified.

Because you are sensitive you must pay the price. But remember always the greatest force in the world, the perfect love of the Great Spirit, is yours and can flow through you. I ask you to trust the counsel of the wisest of the wise, those whose hands direct you, whose power sustains you, who will guide you always out of the storms and difficulties of the world of matter into the haven of peace.

Remember, it is better for your sake if you sit. The power must be used. I say that because I understand the power of the spirit. It must not be bottled up.

You live in a world of light and shade. It is not like that in my world. When you are in the shadow you forget the light, and when you are in the light you forget the shadow. When the snow falls you say it is too cold. When the sun shines you say it is so hot. You want it to snow when the sun shines and you want the sun when the snow falls. Do not let your eyes look down towards the earth, but up towards the sun always.

You cannot be a medium in the highest sense until you have tasted the sorrows and the sweets of your earthly world. You must try to remember that when it looks black it is only the shadow, which passes away. The rays of the sun will enable the gold of your own self to shine once more.

THE LAW OF SERVICE

Spirit guides always stress the importance of service, which they regard as the leading factor not only in individual evolution but in the dawning of the New World. And they practice service as well as preach it!

WE are here to serve. If we can raise up one, if we can mend a broken body, if we can put new courage into a dejected soul, if we can bring new hope, new faith, if we can cause a smile to appear where only tears flowed before, then we render service to the Great Spirit, and we thank Him because we have the instruments of matter through whom we can reach His broken children.

You cannot be weary of service. There is no joy like the serving of one another. You cannot be spent in service. We ask for no praise for ourselves. We seek but to serve the Great Spirit through the operation of His laws, and to show your world of matter that harmony, health, and happiness can be brought through their use.

I strive to serve all I can, to bring what little illumination I can, to help you to learn the real lessons of life, so that, fortified by the knowledge of the spirit, you may fit yourselves for the tasks which are given into your hands to perform.

We render service for service.

Any call to us, any appeal, never goes unanswered. We are here to serve. These are not idle words. They convey an intense reality. We strive to serve because only through service can we express the Great Spirit and only through service can you express the Great Spirit.

Theologians have made out of religion a great mystery, a superstructure of words and doctrines that bring doubt and perplexity and confusion, and yet the essence of all religion and the desire of all life is expressed in the one word "Service."

He who strives to forget self and to serve is expressing the Great Spirit. Service—that is what your world needs today. That is why we strive to teach it and, more, to give it. Try to remember that behind all the mists and darkness, behind all doubts and fears, behind all sorrow and strife, behind all bitterness and pain, there is an eternal purpose. Strive to get an understanding of the greater purposes of life.

You are never alone, you are never left to fight difficulty by yourself. Unseen, unheard, unfelt, the influence of the spirit is always round and about you. Your world of matter could be transformed if it did but understand the realities of the spirit.

We are not angels of darkness, seeking to lead you into paths of confusion. We strive to teach you the simple truths of the spirit that will give you understanding, confidence, peace and happiness. We strive to reveal the knowledge of those laws which can bring you closer to the Great Spirit. That is our mission.

You are servants of the Great Spirit, seeking to make His will done on earth through your labours. In that work there is much happiness, because you are bringing into the lives of many a new hope that was not there before. You are helping the power of the spirit to descend in greater force and therefore you are helping the Great Spirit's laws to operate. You are helping to drive away all the sadness and misery of your world of matter.

The power that is behind you is the power of the Great Spirit of all life, the greatest force in the universe. That power must manifest and you can help it to bring its force into your world. It does not matter what you do—whether you raise one up, whether you give a word of encouragement, whether you serve in the things of spirit or the things of matter—as long as you serve and you are not weary of service, you are instruments of the Great Spirit.

While there is so much misery, strife and discord, while there are tears where there should be happy laughter, while there is starvation, lack of work, poverty in the midst of plenty, how necessary it is for us to continue to express the same truths—the only truths which can free the children of the Great Spirit.

How can you serve the Great Spirit except by serving His

children? Your world is afraid of words, of names, of labels. I call it service. You call it politics, economics, sociology. But these are only words. Wherever you give service, that is your religion.

It matters not whether it is among those who are exalted in your world or among those who are lowly. If you can raise up one soul, if you can bring light to one who is in darkness, if you can free one from the prison-house of ignorance, if you can give food to those who are hungry and water to those who are thirsty, if you can bring peace instead of war, you are serving the Great Spirit.

GUIDANCE FROM BEYOND

Though Silver Birch dislikes speaking of himself, because he considers the message to be all-important, he has sometimes hinted at the great sacrifice made by himself and other guides in sacrificing the reward of their centuries of evolution in order to assist humanity on earth. He discourages questions about himself, but has answered queries regarding guides generally, from which the following are selected:

ARE there groups of guides working at various levels in all countries?

Yes, there are, but it is always a work that persists by experiment and by effort, because it is not possible to determine beforehand the response that we will get from the instruments which are selected. Sometimes years of work have to be cast aside because the instrument fails to pass all the tests. But in every part of your world of matter, people from my world are at work seeking to exert their influence whenever they find people who can respond.

Do guides work in movements that deal with the advancement of humanity?

There is never one effort for good put out in your world of matter that does not immediately attract from our side those who spur you on. No effort for good is ever lost, for it always brings a response from our world which always stands behind the one who seeks to uplift humanity, who desires to serve humanity and who strives to make the lot of the Great Spirit's children easier.

What would be the relation between guides working in connection with different political movements, such as democratic in one country and dictatorial in another?

Words make you their slaves when they should be your slaves. All that we do is to try to teach the laws of the Great Spirit to all His children, wherever they are and whoever they may be, so that the Great Spirit may be expressed through them. Sometimes it is easy, sometimes it is hard, for all His children are not at the same level of growth. We have to use the material that is at our disposal and do the best we can. We do not think in terms of labels. We only think in terms of service.

Can one have a guide working actively with one, and yet be unaware of his existence?

Yes, there are millions like that, but it is better that people should know, so that they can co-operate with knowledge and not remain in ignorance.

Would knowledge of the guides give them more power?

It enables contact to be made more closely, for knowledge is always to be preterred to ignorance. Who would want to be in the dark when he could have the light? Why be thirsty if you can drink?

Why should a guide confine himself to one particular medium?

How little they know of our methods and the way we work! I have told you of the years I have spent in getting ready for my work through this medium. Must I, in order to satisfy someone in your world, spend the same number of years finding another instrument and starting all over again from the beginning?

Why are mediums who, through force of circumstances, are unable to make use of their psychic gifts, sometimes afflicted with mental depression and nerve trouble?

That is because their psychic gifts are not functioning and their bodies are not in harmony as a result.

WHENCE COMES INSPIRATION ?

This chapter contains Silver Birch's views on inspiration and hypnotism and a striking tribute to Thomas Paine, once described as "a dirty little Atheist".

Inspiration is at once the most common and the least recognized form of mediumship. It is mainly through inspiration that men continue their work after death, by impressing their thoughts on those still in this world, through whom in most instances the actual work must be done. This is Silver Birch's comment on one recently passed on:

HE is now learning how to serve. Those who come to us with the desire to serve are taught how they can influence your world by the power of thought. Much can be done by the intensive thought of those who desire to uplift humanity. We teach them concentration to enable them to help in the fight for the Great Spirit and His truth. Although these people are lost to your world in the physical sense, they are really a new strength to you, because they have joined with us to help you.

There is no eternal sleep, because *we* disturb the dead. There are some who go to sleep because they are taught that that is what will happen. We let them sleep until they wake up. You are taught some funny things in your world. They cannot sleep for ever, though. In any case, who wants to sleep when there is work to be done?

Questions and Answers:

ARE people of a certain craft—for instance, newspaper men—helped by identifiable newspaper men who have passed on?

Yes, nothing is lost in your world or in mine. The talent that expresses itself in your world continues to unfold and evolve in the realm of spirit, and the higher it evolves the more it realizes that it must find an instrument through whom it can express itself. So it always seeks to further its evolution by finding one through whom its powers can be revealed. Sometimes that inspiration is unconscious, sometimes it is known. Sometimes so strong is the impressing personality that the stamp of his character is revealed in the inspiration.

Is that inspiration collective, or is it through one individual?

It is both, because all labour in our world is co-operative. We do not expend our energies except in group service. But each of us has to find the instrument through whom he can best express himself.

If nearly everything is received inspirationally, as we are sometimes told about great poets, painters, etc., where does individual originality begin?

I know nothing about beginnings or endings. The Great Spirit is life, life is the Great Spirit. All the seeds of life have been sown. All that is in the universe, as far as my knowledge takes me, always was and always will be. You are all parts of the Great Spirit, with His spirit embedded within the physical body. In miniature, you are the Great Spirit and have access to all the powers of the Great Spirit, according to the evolution of your soul—that is the range that you can receive of all the power that is within the universe.

So that, whilst you cannot create, you can add to, you can shape, you can build, you can deflect, you can improve, you can beautify, you can combine, and you can do much to make better the world in which you live and the universe of which your world of matter is a very small part. The Great Spirit has provided His children with all the materials and the tools. They can help you to fashion, but they cannot create.

HYPNOTISM—ITS VIRTUES AND DANGERS

How many hypnotists understand the power that is theirs? Influence over the mind of another is an immense power—for good or ill. Here are Silver Birch's answers to some questions on this little-understood subject:

IS hypnotism a good subject for study?

If the man who hypnotizes is of good intent, and desires to use his power for service—then, of course, it is good. The hypnotist is only tapping some of the latent powers of the soul.

What is it that the hypnotist gets in touch with?

The over-self, which is the same as the Great Spirit within. I have often told you that, if you could realize the power within you, and if you would use that power, it would enable you to overcome every difficulty. Those powers can be contacted by development, by attuning yourselves to higher vibrations, by living better lives of service, by raising your spirits. The more you are of the earth earthy, the lower are the vibrations to which you respond. The higher you reach out in self-abnegation, the higher are the vibrations to which you respond and the more the Great Spirit that is within you can express itself.

Is the Great Spirit within a separate entity, capable of reasoning, thinking and acting independently of the conscious self?

No, it is conditioned by that part of the conscious mind which is now expressed through your material body. It is only conditioned in that way while you are living in the world of matter. It is not conditioned under the influence of hypnotism, because the hypnotist is like the gaoler who opens the prison door and allows the prisoner to escape. If the hypnotist is of good intent, he can perform great service, for he can stimulate the divine within. But, also, he can stimulate the animal within. But always remember that the consciousness which you now express is but a very small fragment of the consciousness which one day you will express.

That makes us a little dissatisfied.

Yes, it is good to be dissatisfied. Smug satisfaction is no incentive to progress.

Is hypnotism as an aid to mediumship possible and advisable?

It has been tried, but it has been found that once the guides take charge the power of the hypnotist in your world is at an end, for the medium does not then come within the range of his influence. It is not advisable because once a medium has become subject to spirit power he is outside the influence of the hypnotist. It would be better for him to start his development in séances so that the spirit power can begin gradually to exert its influence over him.

You do not regard hypnotism as a short cut to psychic development?

No, there are no "short cuts". You are dealing with the soul and its faculties, and it has taken many millions of years to bring you to where you are today. It is because your world has tried to ignore the spiritual things that it has brought about so many of its disasters. The things of the spirit require careful nurture and slow growth.

A SPIRIT PRAISES THOMAS PAINE

"The 'villains' of yesterday become the heroes of today," said Silver Birch, when, in 1937, he referred to the bicentenary of Thomas Paine, the famous reformer. He went on:

THIS is the day that your world of matter pays tribute to one who, though he did not realize it, was filled with the power of the spirit, and who strove in his own day to uplift those who were oppressed and crushed, who struggled to raise the weak and the fallen, who fought against all injustice, and strove to teach man his rightful heritage.

Those who were in high places fought against that one man, but, because the power of the spirit moved him, that which he did triumphed over all the difficulties of your world. Though he was despised in his day, though he was rejected and persecuted, his work lives on.

I ask you to learn the lesson of that, for the work you do today is the continuation of that same labour. Though you are obstructed, though you meet with hostility and opposition, it is the same truth that you seek to express. You may not gain recognition from those who should be your allies in the great fight for spiritual and material freedom, but your work will live on because that work is stamped with the seal of divine approval.

For that holy and sacred task we need all people of good will, for we recognize no earthly leaders and do not distinguish between class or nation, race or colour, religion or lack of it. We only see the works, the service, the efforts made to uplift, to help and to succour.

That is the great lesson to learn on this day, when tribute is paid in your world and in mine to one inspired man. Your world thinks only of his service in the past. We recognize that a soul which was filled with the burning zeal to labour for his fellows has not become extinguished, but that since his passing to my world he has continued to render service, and still continues to give service, using all his power to aid wherever he can those who strive to improve the lot of the children of the Great Spirit.

Yours is a strange world. The villains of yesterday become the heroes of today—and often your heroes of today are the villains of tomorrow. Those who are despised in your generation will be eulogized in the generations to come.

How narrow is the view of those who call themselves religious! They construct round their religion a thick wall of creeds, and refuse to permit any but those who agree with them to come into their little walled sanctuary. They say: "Outside the wall are those who are the Atheists. Inside are the elect, the religious ones, those who believe as we do."

But the real man of religion is the one who strives to uplift his fellows, who sees only a wrong to be righted, barriers to be crushed, ignorance to be driven out, hunger to be abolished, slums that must be uprooted. He is the real man of religion, for there is no other way of religion except that a man shall lay down his life in the service of humanity.

I tell you always the same things. I can only give you in a few simple words the spiritual truths that you should know by now. There is nothing new to add to spiritual truth. All that is necessary is that those who dwell in your world should so allow their spiritual natures to function that they will be able to receive more readily the power of the spirit—which, too often, they deny.

THE ETERNAL LINK

What is the soul? Science does not recognize its existence and Orthodoxy does not know what it is. Silver Birch declares it to be a fragment of the Great Spirit, that which links us with God for all time. He also replies to questions on the aura, hauntings, time, lies, lunacy, obsession, plant consciousness, Theosophy and astrology.

WITH what do we control our physical bodies, and where is it situated?

I do not know where it is. I cannot find it. Your men of science think that they can cut up the body and find the soul hidden in one of the corners. Or perhaps it flows through one of the veins, or perhaps it is secreted in one of the organs. There is no part of the body where the soul dwells.

Is the soul within the body?

You cannot speak in terms of within or without when you speak of the soul, for the soul has no within and no without. The soul fills all space. It is consciousness. It is not subjected to the limitations of a body, but can range through all infinity, reaching to its height of evolution. It can span your world of matter in a flash. When you travel in your spirit body to a far-off country, where is your soul? You think in terms of your world's measurements. We have no such difficulties to overcome. There is no space to be bounded by the soul. Our consciousness can function in any part of your world as our will dictates.

What is the difference between soul and spirit?

I do not care what names you give to things. I did not make your dictionaries. The soul, to me, is the Great Spirit within. The spirit is the body through which it expresses itself. But other people use words in other ways.

What is the spirit, apart from its vehicles of expression?

The spirit is that part of the Great Spirit—that which you call God—which expresses itself through successive vehicles as it unfolds higher and higher. We have no knowledge of the spirit apart from its expression, for until the spirit expresses itself we do not know it.

What is our conscience?

It is that part of your soul which discerns between the right and the wrong. It is the balance which enables you to understand that the scale is weighed down on either side. It is the pointer of your soul.

★ ★ ★ ★ ★

What is the aura?

The aura consists of the vibrations set up by the body. There are many auras, but the ones that are known to your world are the auras that surround the physical body and the spirit body. All things have auras, even things which do not have consciousness within them. The aura consists of the vibrations that emanate from the body, and according to the state of the body, so there are different vibrations. Those who can see the auras and can interpret them know all the secrets of the individual.

They can diagnose the health of the individual. They know the state of his soul and his mind's unfoldment. They can tell the evolution of that soul, for it is the aura that enables you all to be read as an open book. Your aura registers all that you have said, all that you have thought and all that you have done. Your aura is your eternal judgment, for there you are showing to those who can see exactly what you are within and not as you show yourselves without.

Do you refer to the aura of the spirit body?

Yes. The aura of the physical body has more to do with physical things, such as the health, the temper or habits. All these things register in different colours.

* * * * *

What causes hauntings in the cases where there is a mechanical repetition of events, such as monks walking the passages of monasteries?

Some hauntings are caused by spirits, but in the cases you mention they are caused by intense concentration on earth, leaving an etheric picture which can still be registered. Usually, however, that which your world calls a ghost is one we recognize as an earthbound spirit.

* * * * *

Is time real or artificial?

Time is not artificial, but it has many dimensions. What is artificial is your measurement of it. Time itself is a reality. It exists. Space exists. But your measurements are not accurate because you view time and space from a limited focus. When you have the knowledge of other factors, then the focus becomes more in line with the truth.

* * * * *

Can a lie, told for a good motive, be justified in the sight of God?

I do not understand what is meant by "in the sight of God." You register on your own souls every deed, every thought, every word, so that you are the result of your own evolution, known to all those who can see with the eyes of the spirit. If you have not done that which is right, in deed or word or thought, then your own evolution suffers as a result.

Does the telling of a lie, for good motives, adversely affect one's evolution?

I do not believe in telling lies. There is a time for silence, but it is always better that the truth shall be known.

* * * * *

Is it possible, through physical disability, for the physical self to act in an entirely contrary manner to the desire of the spiritual self?

Yes, as in the case of lunatics, but that does not affect the evolution of the soul. It only affects its expression in the world of matter. You must always allow for a difference between a soul's evolution and its limited expression in your world.

* * * * *

Is it possible for a man who lived a wicked life on earth to remain unrepentant in the spirit world?

Yes, it is quite possible. There are many who do for hundreds and sometimes thousands of years.

Could such a person influence one on this earth to his detriment?

If there is an attraction between them. Your world must learn that obsessions are not caused by our world but by yours, for you provide the conditions. If your lives were lived in conditions of harmony and right thinking, in service and not for self, for greed and only for personal desire, then it would be impossible for obsessions to happen.

* * * * *

Have flowers and plants consciousness?

Not as you understand it, but they have response to vibrations which your world does not yet understand. There are many who can use these vibrations and succeed with flowers and vegetables and plants because they have sometimes by accident found the secret of those vibrations.

* * * * *

What is your reply to the Theosophist teaching that at death the "divine principle" of a man leaves his astral and mental bodies, as well as his physical body, and these remain as empty shells to roam in the earth's atmosphere? The Theosophist teaching is that it is from these shells that communications are received through mediums, the shells being animated by elementals and nature spirits that imitate the characteristics of the dead people.

When a portion of the Great Spirit withdraws from the body of matter, the work of that body is finished and it goes back into the earth. When, in the next stage of life, the Great Spirit withdraws from the astral body, then the work of that body is finished and it resolves itself once more into the elements of which it was composed; for when the Great Spirit withdraws, the life is withdrawn also.

* * * * *

Is astrology a reliable science and useful to man?

Everything in the universe vibrates, and vibrations from all things are constantly being radiated into the universe. All vibrations send out rays and all these rays carry influence. A knowledge of vibrations will always help, for there is a law behind them all.

Is there any relation between similar messages given through spirit guidance and astrological forecasts?

There are millions of ways of expressing truth, because truth is of the Great Spirit and it can only be expressed according to the evolution of the individual through whom it has to be expressed. It is through simplicity that you learn truth. Using long words and finding new names does not make for truth. Often, they serve as masks for ignorance.

"OH, GREAT WHITE SPIRIT . . ."

No book dealing with the teachings of Silver Birch would be complete without one of his invocations. Every week he opens the circle with a beautiful prayer, stressing the same truths but always couched in different phrasing. This one is typical and has not previously appeared in print:

I PRAY to the Great White Spirit that we may be enabled to reveal the operation of the laws that belong to the spiritual realms. I pray that we may be enabled to give a clearer understanding of the Great Spirit and His relationship to all the phenomena of life and to all His children who dwell in the universe.

The Great Spirit has been so misunderstood throughout the centuries, misinterpreted, limited and restricted that we seek to reveal the Great Spirit as perfect law in operation. The Great Spirit is responsible for every manifestation of life. All that exists does so because of His power and His sustenance. The whole order of creation pays tribute to His Law. The mightiest and the lowliest, the strongest and the weakest, the birds, the flowers, the trees, the wind, the ocean, the mountain, the hills and the vales, the sunshine and the rain, the storm and the lightning—all these are but expressions of the Great Spirit of all life.

We seek to reveal that all are fashioned in His spiritual image, that His spirit manifests through their being, that they move and breathe and live because the Great Spirit is within them and they are within the Great Spirit. None has the power to come between the child and the Father, for all the inspiration, all the truth, all the wisdom, all the revelation, all the knowledge that belongs to that infinite reservoir can be reached by each child of the Great Spirit as he desires, in aspiration, humility and service, to become an instrument for that mighty power.

We seek to reveal the greatness latent within every human soul, the mighty force waiting to be released, pent up through misunderstanding, waiting to surge through the physical being and express spiritual heights in their daily lives. We would seek to make all children live lives in fullness, in beauty, in understanding of the purpose for which they were born, so that they might extract from life all the richness, all the sweetness, all the beauty that is theirs for the asking.

We seek to bring the Great Spirit closer to His children and His children nearer to the Great Spirit, to overcome all the obstacles that stand in the way, to banish all the restrictions and limitations so that the children of His world of matter may know the Great Spirit and seek to reveal Him in service. That is the prayer of Thy Indian servant, who seeks to serve.

At the conclusion of every circle, the guide gives the sitters a benediction, always reminding them of the "cloud of witnesses" with which they are surrounded and stressing the inherent divinity of us all. Here is one such benediction:

I WANT you to know that we are close to you, even when you cannot hear us, even when it seems that we are invisible, unseen, unheard, unfelt.

We are around and about you because we love you, and the love that we have for you makes us always seek to serve you and, through you, those who require service—the weak ones, the ones who have lost their strength, the ones who have fallen by the wayside, the derelicts of your world, the weary and struggling souls who do not know where to turn, who can find no comfort in the religion of earthly churches but who have a yearning for truth, those whose souls seek expression but who are choked by the creed and the dogma and the teaching of opposing sects.

The truth that we teach is the truth of the Great Spirit that knows no bounds and no limitation. It is for all, not for one. It seeks to embrace the whole of humanity within its loving embrace.

May you become conscious of that mighty power that is around and about you, of the great love that is always being poured into your world, the inspiration that seeks to express itself through you, the truth that is waiting to be revealed, the wisdom that seeks to illumine your world, and may you strive through service to make yourselves accessible to the mighty power of the spirit, so that you may become at one with the great Force, the Great Spirit, that is behind it all, so that, working in unison with His laws and filled with His knowledge, you may become instruments of His servants for all His children. May the Great Spirit bless you all.

"A LITTLE CHILD SHALL . . ."

This chapter presents Silver Birch in a different light. The reader is acquainted with this guide as a teacher, as a bringer of comfort and encouragement and as a merciless critic of man-made dogma. Now read of his gentleness and simplicity with children. This chapter, written by Paul Miller, is reprinted from "Psychic News".

TWO little children sat on the knees of Silver Birch's medium and talked with the spirit as though he were a lifelong friend. They agreed to ignore the adults in the circle, and the questions and answers from the beloved guide made for the children a picture of the spirit world of great beauty.

These children, Ruth, a girl of eight, and Paul, a boy of six, had prepared a list of questions that the guide had forecast would be harder to answer than most of the problems put to him by grown-ups. It was the first time they had seen anyone being entranced, but it had been explained to them that the medium would go to sleep and that the guide would take possession of his body.

As the medium was overshadowed their bright eyes were fixed on his face as though they could see a change coming over it. Later, when they asked him how he looked, Silver Birch asked them to stand back a little and watch while he transfigured the medium's face. The change in appearance was striking.

"You are different from the medium!" said the little boy.

"You are beautiful!" said his sister, who declared almost as soon as the guide began with his blessing: "What a beautiful voice you have!" To her that was most important, for she forms estimates of character by voices.

What was the purpose of the sitting? It was at the request of the guide that it was held, for he has repeatedly told the parents of the children that the girl is very psychic and has explained that she must be watched carefully for her powers would soon begin to manifest. He has even forecast the first spirit she will see.

"Oh, Great White Spirit," said the guide in his invocation, "may we be able to approach Thee with the simplicity of the child's heart and mind and learn those great truths that are revealed only to those who have the perfect trust of children in a loving and all-wise Parent. May we learn to approach Thee without fear, knowing that Thou art perfect wisdom and love and kindness."

When the guide had asked the little ones to sit, one on each knee, with his head nestling against theirs, he said to them: "I have brought some real fairies for you to play with, and I am going to leave them with you so that they will watch over your beds all through the night and keep you company.

"I am going to try to make you see them, for they are real fairies, not out of books, but out of the fairy kingdom. We will not talk to the big children tonight; we will pretend they are not there. You know, I often come to play with you and bring my own little wigwam."

"What is a wigwam?" asked Paul.

"You call it a tent," the guide replied. "When I lived on earth as an Indian I lived in a wigwam."

"You have such a beautiful voice, and I can hear you so easily," said Ruth.

"This is my voice and not the voice of my medium. I make it specially."

"How do you talk in spirit land?" was her next question.

"We don't speak. We send our thoughts out to each other

on little wings, and they fly quickly through space carried by the stars. And then we receive other thoughts in reply, so that we do not have to find words. When we have a beautiful picture in our minds we can send it at once. We have so many beautiful things here; many more than you have—trees and flowers and birds and streams. Whenever we want a beautiful picture we can make it immediately for ourselves. We can make everything we need."

Then the girl asked whether the guide would help a neighbour who had passed that week and who had been aided by Silver Birch and his band during an illness that invariably ends in great pain. She asked that the two children left behind should be cared for by the Great Spirit. The guide said he had already helped and would look after them.

"Will he be a great spirit like you?" asked Paul.

"Yes, but it will take some time—a few hundred years."

"That is a long time," was Ruth's comment.

"Does it seem a long time to you? No, you get used to it, and then even a long time seems like a little time," the spirit replied.

"How long is it since you were born?" was her next question.

"I have been in the spirit world nearly 3,000 years—and I am still very young."

"I don't call that very young," she said, and added: "When we die will we become spirits?"

"You are little spirits growing up to become big spirits."

"But we are not the same as you," Paul said.

"We are all children of the Great Spirit you call God, and as all the little parts of the Great Spirit are linked together we are one family of the spirit."

"God must be very big," was the boy's next comment.

"He is as big as the whole wide world. And there is much that you cannot see."

"But did God make the Great Spirit?" was his next question.

"He did not make it, for God *is* the Great Spirit Who is always there."

"Does He ever come to earth?" Ruth inquired.

"Yes, He comes to earth every time a baby is born, for then He puts a part of Himself into it."

When the children said that they were glad they believed in spirits, the guide replied that they were very lucky children. "You are fortunate," he said, "because you know you are surrounded by the light and love from those who have passed from your world to mine. They are protecting you always."

"Is your world bigger than ours?" was Ruth's next question.

"Yes. It is much, much bigger and it contains many more beautiful things than you have in your world—such beautiful colours, such wonderful music, such great big trees, and flowers and birds and animals."

"Do you have any animals?" Paul asked.

"We have animals, but they are not wild."

The boy then said: "I don't expect you kill them as you used to when you were on earth."

"We don't kill anything at all."

"Do you get hungry?" he asked.

"No, never, because we are surrounded always by life, and when we get a little tired, we just breathe in more life. When you go up to your little bed at night you stand up and breathe in air, and when you do that you also breathe in life."

Then the children talked about not being able to remember their life in the spirit world, and they added that it seemed like their first life on earth because they could not remember any other existence.

Ruth next asked: "How many lives do we have?"

"You have as many lives as a cat. You know that in your world a cat is said to have nine lives."

"And then does it change into something else?" was the boy's eager query.

"No, a cat is always a cat, but it becomes a more beautiful cat, just as little children coming from your world into mine grow more beautiful the longer they are here. We have no ugliness, no cruelty, no darkness, no fear in our world, which is always a land of sunshine."

This puzzled Paul. "No rain! No rain!" he said. "But if we don't have rain in our world we die."

"But your world is very small. It is only the beginning of life. There are lots of other worlds. There are other worlds in the stars and in the planets where other children live."

Ruth then surprised her hearers with these words: "In *Psychic News*, it says 'All Worlds Are One' " (a reference to a weekly heading of comments in *Psychic News*).

"That is true, but you must know that there are millions and millions of worlds, and there are millions and millions of children, and they are all children of the Great Spirit. They are all one in the Great Spirit, and He is in all."

"Are you tired of speaking?" she then asked.

"No, no. I can speak for a long time yet."

"When shall I see with my spirit eyes, if I have them?" was her next question.

"You have spirit eyes and ears, hands and fingers, and legs with spirit toes, for you have another body—that is the body of the spirit. You can see with your spirit eyes now, but you do not remember what you see while you are in the little physical body you have now. But gradually you will be able to catch what you have seen and hold it."

"Will my spirit eyes be ever so big?" she asked.

"It does not matter, for the eyes of the spirit can see ever so far."

"Can they see right over the world?" Paul inquired.

"They are very like a telescope which can bring distant things into the range of your vision."

Like a bolt from the blue came the boy's next question: "Is there going to be another war?"

"There is always a little war going on, but you don't have to worry about it. You have to think of peace and send the thought from your little mind out into the great world stream of peace and swell its note so that all men in their hearts will desire peace and that will help them to push war away."

Then Ruth asked: "When can I see you properly?"

"You will have to wait a little. You see us very often, but you do not remember. When you go to sleep I take you by the spirit hands. Both of you leave your little earthly bodies asleep on your beds and we travel in my world and we have such wonderful adventures. But when you get back to your body you forget them. You just say what a funny dream I have had."

"But I don't know where I have been," declared Ruth.

Here Paul said: "Sometimes I don't have dreams at all."

"I think you do, but you forget them."

"When you go to the spirit world, do you forget?" asked the girl.

"Yes, the longer you are in the spirit world, the harder it is to remember what happened in your world."

Then unexpectedly the boy said: "I wonder why men kill animals."

"Because they have not yet learned it is wrong."

"Some men feed animals just to kill them," Ruth remarked.

"You try to live without eating animals," said the guide.

"It is cruel to kill animals and eat them," was Paul's contribution.

"It is always wrong to kill anything. Never kill at all."

"Can you speak to people when the medium is not there?" was his next question.

"Oh, yes. I spoke to Swaffer when he went to America though my medium was in this country."

"How nice it must be in the spirit world!" said the girl.

"It is very, very nice. We have nothing that is ugly or dark or miserable. We have such beauty, such splendour."

Still fascinated by the spirit's voice Ruth said: "You really have a beautiful voice, I think," while her brother chimed in with: "I think it is rather unusual."

Then the children, as though they were talking to a playmate, went on to talk like little philosophers that it was a good thing people had different voices, the boy remarking that if we were all the same it would be a very dull world.

The guide broke in to say that though we were all different we were also all the same, because we were all parts of the Great Spirit. Some people, he said, had big spirits in little bodies, and some had big bodies with little spirit.

That gave the boy the idea for his next question, for he asked if there were any dwarfs in the spirit world. Silver Birch explained that there were none in his world, but when they came from the earth they began to grow up.

Then after the girl had asked whether all spirit guides were the same, and whether they were all the same as he, Silver Birch asked them to stand back while he transfigured his instrument's features, so that they could see the difference between the face of the medium and his guide.

Later they told the grown-ups that the guide had a longer face than the medium, and that he had a sharp chin, while the medium had a round one. The girl said that while the change was taking place she saw a light shining from the medium's face.

When they returned to his knees, the boy, usually very shy, said as he nestled in the guide's arms: "I love you."

In answer Silver Birch said: "The Great Spirit is full of such love—such love as there is between us."

"I hope I shall always believe in spirits all my life," said Ruth.

"You will," answered the guide.

The boy asked whether the fairies brought by the guide were all of one colour.

"Some are green, some are yellow, some are blue and some are of colours you have not even heard of," was the reply. "Try to have a look at them just before you go to sleep. They will be with you all night. I will leave them to watch over you while you sleep.

"And now," said the guide, "I want to tell you something before I go. In a very short while, I travel away from this world of yours and I go back into the spheres to be at a great festival we hold at Christmas. There many spirit guides come together and we are spoken to by one you call Jesus, a great lover of children."

Here the guide's moving words were broken off by the little boy who wanted to know if heaven was in the sky.

"No," answered the spirit. "It is here around you, though you cannot see it with a telescope, nor with your earthly eyes."

He went on with his talk. "And when I have left your world just before Christmas I will meet Jesus and I will tell him that I know two little children on earth, one named Ruth and the other named Paul, and I will give Jesus their love."

He continued by describing the festival. "The guides meet, having left their mediums behind," he said. "We take counsel and learn of the things we have done and tried to do. We get a new outlook, and perhaps new wisdom, perhaps even more love and faith and power to take to your world when we continue our work."

Almost like a shot came the question of the boy: "What is wisdom?"

"It is what you know," was the answer, almost as though the question had been anticipated.

Placing a hand on each little head the guide, whose words had struck wonder into the grown-ups and made them silent listeners of the free, frank and loving talk between a great soul and two children, left them with this blessing:

"I bless you in the name of the Great White Spirit Who is love and wisdom and beauty and truth. I pray that you will retain through the whole of your earthly life that simplicity which enables you to be in the kingdom of heaven now. I pray that you will respond to the influence that is now round and about you and that you will become instruments of the Great Power we seek to serve."

Now it was the little girl who asked: "Where is heaven?" and drew an answer that brought tears to the eyes of the sitters.

"Heaven is in your hearts when you are happy," Silver Birch declared.

"It is not in your heart when you are unhappy," said the girl.

"You need never be unhappy," the guide said. "You can always be in heaven when you want to. I am always with you and I try to help you. If you ever forget and cry, I will come and wipe away your tears and bring back the laughter to your eyes that you may grow in happiness."

"You are very kind to us," said the girl, but was met with silence for Silver Birch had left his medium . . .

DEBATE WITH A MINISTER

"I am certain I was not talking to any of the sitters. There was beyond doubt some other entity present—and he knew his Bible, too." These remarks were made by a Methodist minister who, while attending a conference in London, was invited to meet Silver Birch and to submit to him any questions he desired. After the first sitting, the minister was so intrigued that he wanted another talk—and the next time he prepared his questions beforehand. This chapter presents a new facet of the Silver Birch personality, for the guide is disclosed as a debater of no mean order.

HUNDREDS of Methodist ministers, old and young, were gathered at their annual conference at the Central Hall, Westminster. They had been discussing every aspect of their teaching, and work, for nearly two weeks.

Now and then, though only in conversation, "Spiritualism" had cropped up. One Methodist minister, who called on Hannen Swaffer, asked how he could go to a séance. He had read Doyle's book, *The New Revelation*, but, otherwise, he knew little.

"You can come to my home circle tomorrow night," said Swaffer. "During the sitting, Silver Birch, one of the guides, will control a trance medium. You can ask him any question you like, argue, contradict, differ—say anything you please. But do not go away afterwards and complain that something was not explained to you. You can ask anything. We will print the story, but omit your name. Then you will not get into a row, unless you want to."

The parson, a charming, most intelligent young man

obviously imbued with the love of service, went to the séance. In due course, Silver Birch came through.

"May the inspiration of the Great White Spirit dwell among you all," he began, "and may you all respond to all that He would have you do, so that each one of you may feel you are a part of the Great White Spirit. Take that part with you wherever you go, and show it to all the children of the Great White Spirit."

Then, addressing the parson, he explained: "My medium is filled with the power of what you call 'the Holy Spirit.' That makes him 'speak in tongues.' . . . I am one of those who have already been 'resurrected.' "

"What do you think of the other world?" asked the clergyman, beginning his search for knowledge of spirit teaching.

"It is very much like your world," was the reply, "except that our world is a world of effects, and yours is a world of causes."

"Did you have any fear when you left this world?"

"No. All we Red Indians were psychic, and we understood it was nothing to be afraid of. We were psychic like the man who founded your religion—Wesley. He was moved by the power of the spirit. You know that?"

"Yes," said the minister.

"But they do not move by the 'power of the spirit' now," went on the guide. "There are many links in the chain which leads to the Great White Spirit, and the lowest ones in your world are linked to the highest angels, as you call them, in the world of spirit. No one in your world is so bad that he is not in touch with the Great White Spirit, Whom you call God."

"Do you know one another on the Other Side?" asked the Methodist.

"How do you know them in your world?" was the reply.

"With my eyes," said the parson; "I see with them."

"But you do not see with your physical eyes," persisted the guide. "You see with the spirit."

"Yes," admitted the minister. "I see with my mentality, which, I suppose, is part of the spirit."

"I see with my spirit, too," explained the guide. "I see your spirit, and I also see your physical body. But that is only a shadow. The light is the spirit."

"What is the greatest sin people commit on earth?" asked the Methodist.

"There are many, many sins," was the answer; "but the greatest sin of all is the sin against the Great Spirit."

"Tell him what that means," interposed a sitter.

"It is those who know, and deny the Great Spirit," explained the spirit. "That is the biggest sin of all."

"That is what they call 'the sin against the Holy Ghost,'" said one of the circle.

"They call it 'the sin against the Holy Ghost' in the big book," replied the guide; "but it is really the sin against the spirit."

"What do you think of the Revised Version?" asked the parson. "Which is better, the Revised or the Authorized?"

"The words do not matter," said the guide. "It is what you do, my son, that counts. The truth of the Great White Spirit is found in many books, and also in the hearts of those who try to serve Him, wherever they are, and whoever they might be. That is the greatest Bible of all."

"Suppose they do not get converted before they die?" asked the clergyman. "What happens then?"

"I do not understand what you mean by 'converted,'" said Silver Birch. "Put it more plainly."

"Suppose a man lives a wicked life, and passes on," said the minister. "Another man makes a mental resolve to do right. What will the difference between the two men be in the other realm?"

"I will tell you from your own book," said the spirit. "That which a man sows, that shall he reap! You cannot change that. You bring into our world what you are—not what you think you are, and not what you try to show other people you are. It is what you are inside. You will be able to see it for yourself when you come here."

"He dreams dreams," said the guide, meaning the parson, to Swaffer.

"Do you mean he is psychic?" asked Swaffer.

"Yes," was the answer. "Why did you bring him here?"

"Oh! he called on me," said Swaffer.

"He is being led step by step," said the guide, "and the light must be shown gradually."

To the parson, the guide added: "Are you surprised that an old Indian knows so much about your Bible?"

"You seem to know a lot about it," said the Methodist.

"He has been dead three thousand years," said one of the circle.

"Did you know David?" asked the parson, making a quick sum in his head. David lived about B.C. 1000.

"I am not a white man," said the guide. "I am a Red Indian. I lived in the mountains of the North-West of America. I am what you call a savage. But I have seen in your western world more savagery and cruelty and ignorance than ever I saw among the humble Indians three thousand years ago. All the cruelty that the white people practise, even today, on those who are economically worse than themselves, is one of the greatest sins against the Great White Spirit."

"How do you find the people on the Other Side?" asked the parson. "Do they feel remorse acutely?"

"What men are most sorry for is that which they have left undone," explained the spirit. "When you come into our world, you will see for yourself. You will see everything you have done and everything you have not done which you ought to have done. You will look at those neglected opportunities, and that will cause your remorse."

"What do you say about faith in Christ?" asked the minister. "Is that something which satisfies God? If you have faith in him you try to follow his example."

"Not those who say 'Lord, Lord,' " quoted the guide, "but those who *do* the works of my Father. That is all that matters —not what you say or believe, nor even what you think, but what you do. If you have no faith at all, and you help to uplift the fallen, to give bread to the hungry, and light to those who grope in darkness, then you are doing the work of the spirit."

One of the sitters asked whether Jesus was part of the Godhead.

"The Nazarene was a great master, who came into your world," explained the Indian spirit. "They did not listen to his teaching. They crucified him. They are still crucifying him. There is a part of the Great White Spirit in everybody, but in some more of the Great Spirit shows than in others."

"Christ is universally admitted as being the best man who ever lived," said the parson. "Such a man could not lie. He said: 'I and my Father are one. He that hath seen me hath seen the Father.' Did not that indicate that he was God?"

"You must read the Bible again," came the reply. "He said: 'My Father is greater than I,' didn't he?"

"Yes," admitted the parson.

"Didn't he also teach you to pray and say 'Our Father which art in Heaven'? He did not teach you to pray to him. If he taught people to pray to his Father, how could he be his 'Father which art in Heaven'? He did not say: 'Pray to me,' but he said: 'Pray to our Father.' "

"He spoke of 'your God and my God,' " said the clergyman. "He never spoke of '*our* God.' He never put himself on a level with other men."

"He never said 'your God and I,'" persisted the guide. "He said: 'Greater things shall ye do than I do.' You must understand that, when you read your book, you must not try and make the words fit. You must read them with the understanding of the spirit, for the spirit is the key which unlocks all the mysteries. That is why the Nazarene spoke in parables."

Then the parson quoted the words: "God so loved the world that He gave His only begotten son," in support of his contention that the Nazarene was part of the Godhead.

"The Nazarene never said that," said the guide. "It was put into the Bible many, many years after at what you call the Council of Nicea."

"The Council of Nicea?" asked the parson.

"It was in the year 325," answered the spirit, very quickly.

"Those words that I quoted," said the parson, "were in the Gospel of St. John, which was circulated before then."

"How do you know?" asked the guide.

"Oh, history tells us," replied the parson.

"Which history?" persisted Silver Birch.

"I cannot quite tell," said the visitor.

"How do you know?" asked the spirit again. "Where are the books from which your Bible was written?"

"John's Gospel was a finished piece of work," said the Methodist.

"No, I mean before then," replied the guide.

"It was finished by about the year 90," said the visitor.

"Where are the originals from which your Bible was compiled?" demanded the spirit.

"There are various documents," said the minister, naming one of them.

"They are copies," said the guide. "Where are the originals?"

The parson could not answer this, so the spirit guide answered it for him.

"The originals of your book," he said, "are locked up in what you call the Vatican, and they have not been shown to your world. That which you call the Bible is only a copy of a copy of a copy, and in these copies there are many things which are not in the originals. The early Christians expected the Nazarene to come back on his second visit very quickly, so no one wrote down the details of his life on earth. Later on, they lost their hope and their faith, and they started writing down from memory all they could remember. When you say: 'The Nazarene said'—you do not know he said these things."

"Is it not a fact," asked the Methodist, "that there is evidence in the four Gospels of a basic Gospel, which we know as 'Q'? The main facts are in all the Gospels."

"I do not say these things did not happen," said the guide. "I only say that you cannot say every word in your Bible is what the Nazarene said. You must understand that many things in the Bible came from books which existed a long time before the Nazarene came into your world."

"What do you think about the book which is being written on the unwritten sayings of Christ?" asked the minister.

"It is not his sayings that the Nazarene wants," persisted the spirit. "He wants all the people in your world to try and *do* the works of the Father. They worry too much about sayings, and not enough about doings. Where you preach what you call the Gospel, you have a congregation hungering for the truth of the Great White Spirit. It is not what the Nazarene said that counts: it is what you can show in your own life as an example.

"Your world will not be saved by sayings. It will not be saved by long, long words. It will only be saved when the children of the Great White Spirit are ready to gird on the armour of the Great White Spirit and fight the forces of darkness and oppression, all that which holds man in bondage.

That is more important than the unwritten sayings of the Nazarene."

"Why do we get so much pain in this world?" asked the parson.

"It is only through pain that you learn the truth of the Great White Spirit," was the reply. "Out of the crucible of bitter experience you understand the truth of the laws which govern your world."

"Many people seem to have no pain," said the visitor.

"You are a man of God," replied the guide, "and you must learn to understand that it is the things of the spirit that count, and not the things of the body. The pain of the spirit is greater than the pain of the body."

"The present system does seem unfair," said one of the circle.

"One day," was Silver Birch's reply, "everything that happens in your life will be adjusted. One day you will hold in your own hands a pair of scales and adjust the balance yourselves. You cannot escape the natural law that you reap what you sow in this world. You think some get off lightly. But they do not. You cannot see inside their souls.

"The Law of the Great White Spirit is the only law that I recognize. I do not recognize the laws of man. The laws of man have to be altered, and changed, but never the laws of the Great White Spirit. Unless your world is suffering, you are not able to call attention to all the things that you must put right. All the pain and the suffering and the evil are there because you, who are parts of the Great White Spirit, must learn how to overcome them.

"Unless you do these things, you are not doing the works of the Father, Who sent you here. Who are you to judge the Great White Spirit, Whose laws have governed all the world from the beginning, and will go on to the end?"

"What do you do in your world?" was the next question.

"What do you do in this world?" countered the guide.

"Oh, I read a lot," said the Methodist, "and I preach a good deal."

"I read a lot, too," was the guide's answer, "and I am preaching a very big sermon now."

"I have to travel all over the country," said the parson.

"And I have to travel all over the world of spirit," said the guide. "I have to journey down to the dark places where there are people whom your world has sent over here before they are ready. That takes up a lot of my time. I want you to understand that you hold a very great position. Some who call themselves men of God do not fulfil their true function. They merely stand up and speak a lot of words which do not mean anything.

"But if you will put yourself in the hands of the Great White Spirit and open your soul to receive that inspiration which comes from the Great White Spirit's reservoir, you can be filled with that power which inspired the prophets of old. Through your work there can come in your corner of the world a light whose illumination will shed brightness into the hearts of many who are downcast and weary."

"I think that is delightful," said the clergyman.

"No," said the guide. "It is not delightful; it is true. I meet a lot of clergymen here who realize their remorse. They look back and see where they have failed to teach the message of the spirit, where they have concerned themselves about books, words, and sayings, and not enough about doings. They want to come back if they can. I show them how to inspire men like you, so that, through you and others, a new truth of the Great White Spirit may be borne once more in the world.

"You must understand that you live in a world which is falling to pieces, and that you are witnessing the beginning of a new order—a time when the Kingdom of Heaven shall come on earth. It will be accompanied by much pain and suffering and tears, but in the end the Great White Spirit will return to your midst. Each one of you can help to bring the new world into being, for you all are parts of the Great White Spirit, and can help to do His work."

Before the spirit went, at the end of this first séance, he said to the visitor: "I will go with you to your church where you preach. When you preach a very, very good sermon, you will know that it is the spirit."

"I have been praying that I shall have great power," said the parson.

"All your prayers will be answered," was the guide's answer.

* * * * *

"Is it possible for people on earth to live perfect lives, to be sanctified and made holy?" was the minister's first question at the second séance. "Is it possible for us to love everybody?"

"No, it is not possible, but you can try," said Silver Birch. "All the efforts you make are very important in the building of your character. If you never were angry, never bitter, and never lost your temper, you would cease to be human. The Law is that you are put here to develop your spirit, so that it can grow and grow. It never stops growing in your world or in mine."

"What did Jesus mean when he said: 'Be ye perfect even as your Father which is in Heaven is perfect'?"

"He meant you must try to be perfect," replied the guide. "That is the ideal you should try to express in your life—to express the Great White Spirit that is in you."

"The passage I quoted occurs in the last verse of the 5th chapter of St. Matthew," explained the visitor. "It comes after Christ was speaking about universal love, and he said that 'certain people love their neighbours and some people love their friends, but be ye therefore perfect, ye are the children of God.' The idea is that God loves everybody, and we should love everybody. Do you think that Christ would have given us a command which we could not carry out?"

"You want to make all the world like the Nazarene!" exclaimed Silver Birch. "Do you think that he lived a perfect life in your world?"

"Yes, I think he lived a perfect life."

"Do you think he was never angry?"

"I think he was disgusted with certain things that went on."

"Do you think he was never angry?" persisted the guide.

"I think he was never angry in the sense that it is wrong to be angry."

"That is not the question I asked you. I asked you whether he was ever angry; not could you justify it, because you can always justify anything."

One of the sitters recalled the incident when Jesus turned the money-changers out of the temple.

"That is what I meant," said the spirit. "You must not try to read into the life of the Nazarene something that did not happen. He was very angry when he saw people in your world desecrate the temple of the Great White Spirit, and he took whips to whip them out. That was anger. I do not say it was not justified, but it was anger, and anger is a human passion.

"I only tell you that to show you that he had some human qualities. When you try to follow the example of the Nazarene, you must understand that he was a human being in whom there was a great manifestation of the Great White Spirit—a greater manifestation in his case than there has been in other cases. Is that clear?"

"Yes."

"I am only trying to help you. You must not think that the way to please the Nazarene is to put him on a very high pedestal where nobody else can reach him. You please him only when you make him like you and like every other man in the physical world. He does not want to be above. He wants to be with them. He wants to be an example, so that everyone else can do the things he did. If you put him so high that no one in your world can follow him, then all his life is in vain."

"Do you think we have free will?" asked the minister, changing the subject.

"Yes. Free will is the law."

"Don't you think that sometimes a man is made to do things under impulses over which he has no control? Is he impelled to do things, or has he free will?"

"What do you think?" queried the guide.

"I think we are free agents," said the minister.

"You are all given free will," Silver Birch explained, "except that you must live all your lives within the Law of the Great White Spirit. The laws which are laid down by His love, for the use of all His children, are there, and you cannot change them. Within all these limits you are free."

"If we are free, then sin is a terrible thing," declared the visitor. "If a man sins wilfully, it seems more terrible than if he were impelled to do it."

"I can only tell you this: Whatever wrong is done in your world, the one who does that wrong must put it right. If he does not put it right in your world, then he must put it right from our world."

"Do you think that some people have very strong hereditary tendencies in things that are not ideal?" asked the Methodist. "It is easier for some people to be good than others."

"That is a very hard question," confessed the spirit, "because each one of you has free will. When you do that which is not right, inside your heart you know it is not right.

Whether you resist it or not depends on the character which you have grown for yourself. The sin is bad or worse only according to the harm that it does."

This immediately brought the question: "Doesn't that cut across the idea that sin is an intellectual thing? If sin is only bad in relation to its consequences, then sins of thought do not count at all."

"All sin is sin," was the reply. "Whether you sin with the body or the mind or the spirit, it is all sin. You asked just now whether man acts on impulse. Where does the impulse come from?"

"From thought."

"Where do the thoughts come from?" asked Silver Birch.

The minister hesitated and said: "The good thoughts come from God."

"Where do the bad ones come from?" persisted the spirit.

"I don't know."

"The Great White Spirit is in everything," declared Silver Birch, "in that which is wrong and in that which is right. He is in the sun and in the storm; in everything that is beautiful and everything that is ugly. He is in the sky and the ocean, the thunder and the lightning; not only in beauty and goodness, but in sin and ugliness. Do not you understand; you cannot limit the Great White Spirit? The whole world is His creation, and His spirit is everywhere.

"You cannot cut off anything and say that does not belong to the Great White Spirit. You must not say that the sunshine comes from the Great White Spirit and the rain, which destroys the crops, comes from the devil. The Great White Spirit is in everything. You are like an instrument which can receive thoughts and send out thoughts, but the thoughts that you receive depend upon your character and your spirit. If you live what you call a perfect life, then you can only receive the perfect thoughts. But because you are human, you receive all kinds of thoughts—just those thoughts which your soul and your mind are capable of receiving. Is that clear to you?"

"Yes, I think so," was the minister's comment. "Suppose anyone gets on in life and finds that he has received and followed the bad and neglected the good. He is about to pass over and his life is worrying him. What is your opinion of the peace which people profess to experience when they accept the words, 'By faith are ye saved'? What do you think about the doctrine of conversion?"

Without hesitation the spirit replied: "I quote words from your book, which I think you know: 'What shall it profit a man if he shall gain the whole world and lose his own soul?' Then there are some more words which say: 'Seek ye first the kingdom of God, and all these things shall be added unto you.' You know those words well, but do you understand them? Do you realize that they are real, they happen, they are the Law? You know those words which say: 'Whatsoever a man soweth, he shall reap.'

"How can you cheat the Law of the Great White Spirit? Do you think a man who all his physical life has neglected his opportunities to help his fellow-beings, can, on his death-bed, be converted and his spirit alter in one second? Do you think he can blot out all the things which he should have done, which register themselves on his spirit body?

"Do you think that in the sight of the Great White Spirit a man who has neglected his own spirit is on an equal basis with the man who strives all his physical life to work for the Great White Spirit and for His children? Do you think the Law of the Great White Spirit can be just if, because a man says he is sorry, he could wipe out all his sins? Do you think so?"

To this the minister said: "I think that God, in Christ, has provided an escape. Jesus said——"

But Silver Birch interrupted: "My son, I asked you a very

straight question. I want a very straight answer. I do not want you to tell me what it says in a book, because I know what it says there. What do you think?"

"It does not seem fair, but it is just there that the greatness of God's love comes in," said the cleric.

"If you walk down this road, you come to a big building where they administer the laws of man," declared the guide. "If the law were administered as I have just explained it, that a man who sins all his life and the man who tries to do good all his life are equal in the eyes of the law of man, would you say that the laws of man were just?"

"I do not say that the man who has walked in the straight road all his life," the minister replied, "and has loved everybody, and has acted in an upright way, and trusted in Christ all his life, I do not say——"

Again the spirit interrupted: "He sows, and what he sows, he reaps. You cannot escape the Law. You cannot cheat the Law."

"But what message have I got for a dying man if I have to tell him he has made a mess of things and must make up for it?" the parson asked.

"Tell him this from me," Silver Birch answered. "If he is a real man, in whom there is something of the Great White Spirit, then he, as a man, will want to put right all the things which he put wrong. If he wants to escape from the consequences of all his own actions, then I say he is not a man; he is only a coward."

"When a man confesses his sins, don't you think he is doing a thing that not everyone has the courage to do?" was the next question.

"It is only a step in the right direction," said Silver Birch. "But the confession does not wipe out the sin. He had free will, and he chose to do wrong instead of doing right. He cannot escape the consequences. He must put it right. He only cheats himself by thinking he can say a magic formula to gain escape. He must reap what he has sown; that is the Law."

The minister persisted: "But Jesus said: 'Come unto me . . . and I will give you rest'."

The spirit asked the minister if he knew these words: " 'The letter killeth, but the spirit giveth life.' " Then he added: "You cannot take all the words and say that you must accept their literal meaning, because if you do, there are many things in that book which you do not do today. You know that."

Once again the parson quoted: "Jesus said: 'The good shepherd giveth his life for the sheep.' I always preach the doctrine of forgiveness, implying that if a person accepts the forgiveness that Christ offers, and at the same time he tacitly admits that the whole law of Christ governs his life, his life is then one great offering of love."

Then Silver Birch forced home this lesson: "The Great Spirit has implanted in you some of His own reason. I plead with you to use that reason. If you do anyone a big wrong, and you confess it, that confession helps your spirit, but it does not alter the fact that you have done some wrong. Until you have put it right in the eyes of the Great White Spirit, the sin will remain. That is the Law, my son. You cannot alter laws, not even by quoting words from books, which you say the Nazarene said.

"I tried to explain to you before. Not all those words were said by him, but many of them were added afterwards. When you say 'The Nazarene said' you mean you think the Nazarene said those things. What I want you to try and understand is that the same spirit, the same inspiration, the same force of the Great White Spirit which made the Nazarene the great master that he is, is waiting for you, if you open your heart to receive it from the Great White Spirit.

"You are a part of the Great White Spirit. All His love, all His power, all His wisdom, knowledge and truth are there waiting for you. You must not go back into the past for the Great White Spirit. He is here now; just as much the Great White Spirit today as He was in the time of the Nazarene, and the same powers He had then, He has now.

"There are very few instruments through whom He can give His teaching and His power. Why should your Christianity be dependent upon one human being of two thousand years ago? Why cannot all you men of God receive the same inspiration that he did? Why must you go back to what he said?"

"I talk of the work of Christ in me," was the parson's reply. "I believe it is possible to have inspiration."

"Why do you limit the Great White Spirit to the Nazarene and to one book?" inquired the spirit. "Do you think that the whole of the Great White Spirit was expressed in one person or one book? I am not a Christian. I lived many years before the Nazarene came into your world. Did not the Great White Spirit make any allowance for my spirit to enter into His peace?

"Do you think all the Great White Spirit can be put into a few pages in one book? Do you think that when that book was finished, He had no more inspiration for His children? Do you think you have come to the end of His power when you have turned the last page of your Bible?"

"I hope not," said the minister. "I sometimes feel that I am inspired."

"One day you shall go unto the Father also," declared the spirit, "into one of those many, many mansions that you are preparing for yourself in your world today. I want you, who are a man of God, to understand that you cannot limit God, for He is everywhere. The lowest criminal in the lowest haunt of vice is linked with the Great White Spirit as much as the highest saint who ever lived in your world. The Great White Spirit is in each one of you. If you try to express that spirit, and if you will make your heart open, the Great White Spirit will pour through you the power and the revelation that will bring light and comfort to all those who are in your corner of the vineyard."

"How do you explain the fact that the only calendar that has survived to any extent is the Christian calendar?" was the next question.

Silver Birch replied: "Who told you that? Have you not heard of the calendar of the Jewish people? In many other places there are still calendars in existence that date back from the beginning of their own religion. I do not try to belittle the work of the Nazarene. I know the work he does, and I know the Nazarene does not want to be worshipped as the Great White Spirit. The whole value of his life is as an example to be followed. Until the worshipping of the Nazarene stops, there will be little inspiration in your Christianity."

The minister then said: "We cannot find out when it was decided to make the date of Jesus's birth the beginning of the calendar. Can you tell me?"

"I must answer in my own way," said the spirit. "A few days ago, a member of this circle went to the North. There he stayed with many of the children of the Great White Spirit. They are not people in high places. They are men who, if they have physical work, work very, very hard. When they have finished, often after digging deep into the bowels of the earth, they receive as a recompense a few physical pennies. They live in what you call houses, which are a disgrace to your Christian civilization.

"In the same town there is what you call a house of God. This house of God is so tall that the houses near by, when God's sun shines, are in the shadow. They have more darkness in their lives than if the cathedral was not there. Do you think that is right?"

"I used to live in Durham," said the parson.

"I know," was the answer. "That is why I told you."

"I am very sorry that they have to live in those houses," the cleric declared.

"Do you think the Nazarene would be pleased that they should?" said Silver Birch. "Do you think he would ask questions about the calendar as long as there were houses like that, and men who have to work like that, men who only have a few physical pennies, while all the time there are others to whom thousands of physical pennies do not matter?

"Do you think that he would ask for money for cathedrals and ask about calendars and talk about good books when people lived like that? What do you think of a Christianity that goes on using his name and still allows these things to operate in this country that is called Christian?

"You ask questions about texts. Religion has much more important and greater work to do. Do you not see that the Great White Spirit wants all His children to receive His bounty? In some parts of your world they are throwing away the necessities that other people starve for. Can you talk of Christianity while Christians do these things?

"I have a much closer touch with the Nazarene than you imagine. I have seen his tears as he watches, because so many of his people and his ministers close their eyes to all the disgrace which goes on in the shadow of their own churches. How can you be content to build churches which are supposed to be the houses of God, fill them with jewels and stained-glass windows, and boast of the building when all the time, in their shadows, there dwell children of the Great White Spirit who have not even necessities of life?

"Many of them have not even a proper place on which to put their poor tired bodies when they have worked all day and sometimes into the night for a few physical pennies that are not enough for their bread. I do not speak with any bitterness to you. I am only filled with a big love for you, and would do anything to serve you. But I am in the spirit world and have few opportunities of talking to men like you, who can go out into your world and stir up things so that you can put right so much that is wrong.

"I want you to understand there are more important things than texts in the Bible. Not every one that saith, 'Lord, Lord . . . but he that doeth the will of my father.' He taught you that many years ago. Why cannot you make all people see that this is the only thing that matters? It is what you do that counts.

"As long as you countenance all the wars, the iniquity, the starvation, poverty, and unemployment, you are all failing in your Christianity, and you are not following the example of the Nazarene. You have come away from a big conference, where you have joined, in the last twelve months, three sections of your church. Unless when they are united they strive in unity to alter those blots on the Law of the Great White Spirit, your unity is nothing. I speak very frankly to you. I do not want any misunderstanding."

"Some years ago, we threw open our schools and collected money in the churches to provide things for the unemployed," said the minister. "We cannot do everything, but, according to the number of people who go to church, don't you think we try very hard?"

"I know your heart is good," the spirit commented, "otherwise I would not come back to talk to you again. I see in you an instrument which can be of service. The people who go to your churches are very few, but did not the Nazarene teach you to go out into the highways and byways? You must not wait for people to come to you. You must go to them.

"You must make your church a centre of light, and feed not only the souls, but the starving physical bodies. Give them not only words of wisdom, but bread and the necessities of life. You must feed their souls and their bodies. You can help not only the spirit, but the body through which the spirit must function. Unless all the churches do this, the physical bodies will die because they do not get that which sustains them."

The guide then gave the parson a benediction: "I pray to the Great White Spirit that, wherever you are, whatever you do, His power and His love may sustain you; that your heart, always filled with a desire to serve, shall be open to the inspiration of the Great White Spirit. May He infuse into you a greater capacity for service, that you may build around you a centre of light, of peace, of happiness, so that all those who come to that centre may understand that it is a place where the Great White Spirit reigns.

"May He bless you and sustain you and keep you always in His path. May you learn to understand more clearly His purpose, His power, and His plan. God bless you, my son, and go forward."

Complete your collection

All of Silver Birch's books make superb reading, providing inspiration, illumination and perhaps occasionally consolation. Over the years, the guide answered literally thousands of questions on almost every subject imaginable. Below are futrther Siver Birch titles which are available. These can be read and enjoyed either individually or as a complete set, one which makes a unique collection to refer to time and time again. Each volume gives the guide's views on a comprehensive range of topics both here and hereafter.

The Silver Birch Book of Questions and Answers Compiled by Stan A. Ballard and Roger Green. This latest Silver Birch title is in easy-to-read question-and-answer form. It answers literally hundreds of points, such as "Do we reincarnate on earth?", "What are the spiritual aspects of heart transplant surgery?" and "Can euthanasia ever be right?" 240 pages. £7.99

The Seed of Truth Compiled by Tony Ortzen. Based upon two earlier out-of-print titles "Silver Birch Speaks" and "More Wisdom of Silver Birch'" which were compiled by the medium's wife, Sylvia. It contains an account of when actress Mary Pickford, "the world's sweetheart," met and questioned Silver Birch. Each chapter ends with one of the guide's uplifting prayers. 174 pages. £7.50

Lift Up Your Hearts Compiled by Tony Ortzen. This carefully chosen selection of teaching comprises the guide's wise words over a twenty-year period. Animals, a spirit view of death, mediumship and karma are just four of the many subjects explained. Features a verbatim account of when Doris Stokes and Doris Collins, two of Britain's most famous mediums, were addressed by Silver Birch. 229 pages. £7.50

Philosophy of Silver Birch Edited by Stella Storm. A former secretary to Maurice Barbanell and then chief reporter at "Psychic News," Stella Storm covers such issues as natural law, lessons of bereavement, the responsibility of mediumship and "Healing, the greatest gift of all." Silver Birch also tells what he would say to a television audience. This popular book is now in its sixth impression. 155 pages. £7.50

More Philosophy of Silver Birch Compiled by Tony Ortzen. In easy to read question-and-answer form, of special interest are two chapters which trace man from birth to what lies Beyond. Social problems, reincarnation and science are amongst other subjects examined. This title ends with inspiring bite-sized "points to ponder." 253 pages. £7.50

Silver Birch Companion Edited by Tony Ortzen. Drawing upon "More Teachings of Silver Birch" and "Wisdom of Silver Birch," this volume features an account of the night Maurice Barbanell died and the days that followed. Features the replies the guide gave to a Fleet Street editor. 159 pages. £7.50

A Voice in the Wilderness Edited by Tony Ortzen. Most of the material in this book came from handpicked cuttings at the archives of "Psychic News," though it also draws upon the out-of-print "Home Circle" and "Spirit Guidance". Read the advice the guide gave to a Member of Parliament, a senior Army chaplain and delegates at an International Spiritualist Federation congress.
128 pages. £7.50

The Spirit Speaks Compiled by Tony Ortzen. An abridged amalgamation not only of "Silver Birch Speaks Again" and "Anthology of Silver Birch" but also important teachings that originally appeared in "Psychic News". Amongst its highlights is a word-for-word report of a meeting betwen Silver Birch and film star Merle Oberon, who was devastated when her fiancé was killed in a plane crash. 142 pages. £7.50

Guidance from Silver Birch Edited by Anne Dooley. A former Fleet Street journalist, Anne Dooley later became a reporter at "Psychic News", first 'meeting' Silver Birch in 1963. Amongst subjects in this compilation are the problems of suffering and communication with the spirit world. 120 pages. £7.50

Teachings of Silver Birch Edited by A.W.Austen. First published in 1938, this classic Silver Birch title has so far run to seven impressions. It contains a fascinating Foreword by famous journalist Hannen Swaffer, after whom the Silver Birch circle was named. Silver Birch tells his own story and, as usual, answers countless questions, including life in the spirit realms.
243 pages. £7.50

Silver Birch Anthology Edited by William Naylor. Love's supreme power, what happens after we die and "Who if Silver Birch?" are just three of the topics in this absorbing book. Originally published in 1955, the philosophy within this book is still fresh, vital and valuable. 132 pages. £7.50.

Light from Silver Birch Compiled by Pam Riva. Contains the last ever teachings from Silver Birch after the sudden passing of his medium Maurice Barbanell on July 17th, 1981. Also featured is Maurice Barbanell's obituary, which, ever the keen journalist, he prepared in advance. His mission with Silver Birch lasted sixty-one years. Pam Riva was the medium's secretary at "Psychic News", the paper he founded in 1932. 218 pages. £7.50

The Universe of Silver Birch By Frank Newman. This book is unique as Frank Newman has examined Silver Birch's teachings and measured them side by side with the deductions of modern science. This brings important new insights into Silver Birch's philosophy. The result is an intriguing, thought provoking volume.
118 pages. £7.50